Wake Up!

Awaken the Spirit Within and You'll Never be the Same Again

Becki Balok

Becalm Publishing, Inc. Berkley, Michigan

© 1998 Becki Balok

First Edition

Published by:
Becalm Publishing Inc.
P.O. Box 725378
Berkley, MI 48072-5378

Library of Congress Cataloguing-in-Publication Data
Balok, Becki, 1956-
    Wake Up! Awaken the spirit within and you'll never be the same again / Becki Balok.
    128 p. 21.5 cm.
    ISBN 0-9662759-0-X

1. Spiritual Life. 2. New Age Spirituality. I. Title.

BP605.N48   299.93   98-92518

ISBN 0-9662759-0-X
Printed in the U.S.A. on recycled paper
Distributed by Becalm Publishing, Inc.

Dedication

To Rev. Guy Lynch who caught me sleepwalking through life and woke me up!

Contents

About the Author

A Michigan resident, Becki Balok, was born in Highland Park. She attended Guardian Angels Grade School, graduated from Clawson High School (1974), from Hope College (1980, Bachelor of Arts Cum Laude, Geology), from Western Michigan University (1981, Master of Science in Librarianship), and from Wayne State University (1990, MBA).

She worked as a research librarian for 16-years and currently is an analyst at a major automotive manufacturer.

In the Spring of 1986, she presented "A Passion For Excellence" at the Special Library Convention in Boston. She co-authored a paper, "When Career Panic Strikes: Motivation Calms the Fears" published in the September 1991 issue of American Management Association's Personnel magazine. Her essay, "What Are You Clinging To?" appears in the 1997 Church of Today Anthology.

Becki served on the Guardian Angels Parish Council in 1982-3, and there taught Catechism to 6th graders 1984-1986. She has been a member of St. Columban's Parish (Birmingham) since 1988. She joined the Church of Today (Warren) in 1996. She was appointed to serve on Berkley Library Building Committee in 1996. In 1997, she joined the Unity Toastmasters Club and is currently the Vice President of Education. In 1998, she became the President of Becalm Publishing, Inc.

Acknowledgements

An ancient Zen proverb says, "When the student is ready, the teacher will appear". Rev. Guy Lynch "appeared" in my life exactly when I was ready for a change. The spiritual principles he teaches combined with his humorous style not only woke me up but transformed my life. He would often conclude meditations with the phrase, "..and we are already aware that we will never be the same again". Those words resonate deep within me, and I conclude each chapter with them as a tribute to him. Guy is the minister at Unity Chapel of Light and a council member for the Association for Global New Thought. I am eternally grateful not only for his review and input to this manuscript but also for the extraordinary awakened spirit that dwells within him and reaches out to all.

My thanks to Dave Thomas (Thomas International) for his advice and counsel on the logistics of printing and artwork. And to Annabelle McIlnay, who edited this manuscript. I did not make every suggested change, so any "errors" you find are mine.

Foreword

Becki Balok has written a very important book. It summarizes New Thought spirituality in a way that facilitates healing and transformation. I hope this book will show people that they can have a direct relationship with God and that God is loving them in a very personal way.

This book is user friendly and Becki emphasizes the most important points with the phrase "Consider – just consider." When you see these words, it means that Becki is about to challenge traditional thinking and offer alternative thought that can help you build your own spiritual belief system.

Sociologist Paul Ray has established that at least 44 million people would describe themselves as spiritual without being religious. This book has nothing to do with religion. It only describes principles that are spiritual in nature <u>and</u> work practically in our lives. Becki offers them as something to try for yourself. The proof is always in the transformation. Many times from a Sunday pulpit I will say "If Guy Lynch tells you of a principle and you try it in your life and it doesn't work – for heaven's sake, stop doing that." This is exactly the way one should operate with the principles Becki sets forth. We are only interested in what works and I know I can speak for Becki when I say that she is not so interested in being right as she is in facilitating improvement in the quality of peoples lives.

The really great thing about this book is that it is <u>not</u> written by a minister. It is written by someone whose own thought processes have been transformed and who has felt compelled to share by putting pen to paper, or if you will, fingers to keyboard. There are no heavy theological terms to wade through nor is there any detectable bias or leaning toward any particular denomination. She refers to Jesus, but not as the only path to God.

I am delighted with this book because it puts forth New Thought ideas without apology. Marianne Williamson once said, "The problem with America today is not that the voices of darkness are so loud. The problem with America today is that the voices of light are so quiet." Becki has raised her voice of light without establishing any adversarial position nor has she defended her belief by tearing down any other belief. The rest of us need to take note and begin to stand up and be counted as those who are open to spirit and open to the idea that we are spirit.

Reverend Guy Lynch
December 10, 1997

Introduction

Have you ever felt like you are sleepwalking through life? Oh, you get from point A to point B, do all your chores, go to work day-in and day-out, but somehow something is missing. Perhaps you feel like some kind of zombie just going through the motions, counting down to the weekend and waiting for each event just to be over.

Occasionally you realize this state of unconsciousness and decide perhaps you need a change. Perhaps a new job will do it, perhaps a new relationship, a change of scenery. Sometimes you think that if you only had more money, new friends, less weight, a better boss, a bigger house, a better vacation then all would be well. But have you noticed that no matter how much you change the outer parts of your life, something is still missing?

I've discovered that what I perceive of as missing can only be found within. Nothing outside of me, no job, no car, no house, no partner, no boss will ever be more powerful than the spirit within me. The challenge then is to wake up to the spirit within.

I believe the new century will welcome a spiritual renaissance across the country. Those who have been awakened to the spirit within will lead it. Some call this New Age Spirituality, or Transformational Christianity. It is not so new, it is exactly what Jesus and other great masters have taught. But today, many people from all kinds of religious backgrounds and cultures are building the momentum that will usher in the awakening on a global scale.

People like Rev. Guy Lynch, Fr. John Powell, Neale Donald Walsch, Les Brown, Mary Manin Morrissey, Fr. Leo Booth, Bernie Siegel, Deepak Chopra, Wayne Dyer, and many others have changed my life and I am so grateful. I encourage you to read their books, listen to their tapes, attend their seminars.

I believe that each of us has unlimited potential, all things are possible with God. We are forgiven for the worst thing we've ever done because God loves each of us unconditionally. There is nothing we could possibly do so God would love us more. God is within. It is only when I am truly awakened to the spirit within that miracles happen. We are all connected, there is only one power in the universe, and that is God. It is only when we lift up another that we all rise. These are the spiritual principles for the 21st century.

I believe them so strongly, I started to re-read the New Testament to see what my awakened spirit would find. I took some stories I never really understood before and tried to discover their meaning with my newfound spirituality. I took the spiritual principles taught by the people listed above, allowed fresh air to enter the New Testament stories, and wrote this book.

This book, written for all those on a spiritual journey, is about change. It is about looking at the same old "stuff" in a whole new way. It is about renewal and reunion. It is about finding a better way. It is about waking up to the spirit within you.

Begin the greatest adventure of all, the journey inward with a series of 28 questions. I suggest you read one a day, and allow your spirit to transform the principle for your life. Working with the principles on a daily basis will carry you into the 21st century with a renewed sense of purpose, unextinguishable joy, and relationships filled with unconditional love. The new century awaits. Allow this book to reacquaint you with who you really are and re-introduce you to who God really is.

Becki Balok

1
Are You Ready to Start Over?

Not so very long ago,
a single star shown brighter than all
others.
Its light was pure and white,
it twinkled each and every night.

Since the beginning, it travels the sky,
rising each dusk, setting each dawn.
Each night when at its highest peak,
it drops some stardust to the earth
below.

The stardust flies free until it finds
someone needing to start anew.
On this one's head the stardust glitters
though no mortal eyes can see it.

The soul – the spirit dwelling within – is
awakened by such bright light.
Though grumpy at first, for it enjoyed its
slumber, the soul remembers wherefore
it came:
To lead the one on the journey of life,
To teach the one with silent whispers,
To move the one through fear,
To show the one that nothing is
impossible with God.

Many have awakened in just this way.

You've heard of them no doubt
Jesus, Buddha, Gandhi, Mohammed,
the list is much longer but not yet long
enough.

The work of the soul is not yet done and
the star shines ever bright.
Tonight when at its highest peak,
it will drop some stardust to the earth
below.

Will it be you the stardust finds?
Are you ready to start anew?
It is the first step to awakening the spirit
within.
Won't you be open to all the soul has to
teach you?

Your light shines bright, your soul is
awakened.
Lately, your soul has had a bit of trouble
getting through to you.
Not to worry, the soul grows not bitter,
Only more direct and has decided to
write you a letter:

Dear Friend and Companion,

> *Your head is covered with stardust,*
> *The light is very bright.*
> *So bright that I am now fully awake.*
> *That can only mean one thing,*
> *it is time for you to start anew.*

This letter has a four-fold purpose.
There are four things you must do to start anew.
But allow me first to introduce myself:

I am your soul. I am with you always. I walk when you walk. I swim when you swim. I work when you work. I play when you play. I sleep when you sleep. I love when you love. I hug when you hug.

I am your mind. I am your left brain and your right. You can call me conscious or sub-conscious. I am both. I am your real, authentic self. I am your sacred self. I am your higher self.

I am love. I am the spirit that resides within every part of you. I am the part of you, the real you, where God dwells. I am God. I am spirit.

Try as you may, you cannot get rid of me. You can pretend I don't exist, or you may be unaware of my presence, but I am always with you.

I am writing this letter because it is time for you to wake up and start anew. There is so much I need to do through you, and we are running out of time. Now that you are clear about who I am, let us begin the four things you need to start over again:

∞

First, I need you to be open and relaxed. So sit comfortably, and clear your mind, repeat slowly, "I love you". These are the most powerful words in the human language. Oh, not when you say them to another, but when you say them to yourself. Some people wait their whole life to hear that special someone say "I love you". The good news is that you are that special someone. The person you have been waiting for is *you*. So repeat slowly, "I love you". Relax your muscles. Start at the top of your head, un-wrinkle your forehead, close your eyes, drop your jaw, shimmy your shoulders. Make a fist, then think to yourself "I love you, let go, release" as you loosen the muscle. Slowly and gently, tighten then loosen all your muscle groups. Do that over all your muscles from your neck down to your toes.

∞

Second, let go of the past. The past does not exist unless you carry it around. I keep putting it in a vault and throwing out the key, but you keep finding ways to get in, drag the past out, and relive it. You need to let it go; it is the only way to grow.

Start by letting your parents, teachers, family, boss, the president, whomever, off the hook. They did the best they could given the awareness they had at the time (granted their awareness may have been miniscule).

Next, change the mental picture you have of the past (be it something that happened this morning, yesterday, last month, last year, 5-10-20-50 years ago.) Your mind is a marvelous computer, it stores events as pictures - like photographs and your muscles and cells store the emotion associated with those pictures[1]. Storing the emotions can cause chronic physical pain. You can change those pictures, the associated emotions, and be free of pain.

For example, remember some negative event from the past. Picture the entire event, the colors, the temperature, the people involved. Feel the pain, hear the hurtful words, "You'll never amount to much", "You'll never learn", "You shouldn't do that". Now, release and let go of the pain and replace those words with positive ones. "You have great potential", "You have the makings of a genius", "You can do whatever your heart desires". Now, if you must relive the moment, hear these new words. Create a new mental picture. Let go of the hurtful past. Feel the pain dissipating.

Do I sense skepticism? I know, you are thinking - but that is not the way it happened. Now listen carefully. The past does not exist, you are the only one carrying it around. The perpetrator does not remember it so why not make it positive and affirming and get rid of it? Give it a try. What have you got to lose?

Letting go of the "old" past, things you've stored for decades is important, but learning to let go before events get stored is critical. Events, circumstances, and people are influencing you every minute. Realize that none of this "stuff" matters. None of it. All that matters is what you do about the event, circumstance or person. You can choose to be mad or glad, to forgive or be unforgiving, be a doormat or to stand up for yourself, choose to fear or love. It is always your choice. Remember, at every moment you can choose to change your mind, think differently - and let the "stuff" go before it starts to painfully store in your body.

∞

Third, let go of the persistent urge to control someone else's opinion of you. You can't manipulate or control the way others think of you. You want everyone to like you. This is only natural. But, you need to let them be free to feel about you however they choose. Some may really like you, some marginally, some may hate your guts. You cannot control their feelings. You don't need their acceptance. If they choose to reject you, give them their freedom, and move on. You will be fine. Not even you and I together, can make someone love you if they choose not to. Stop trying. It is ok.

One more thing while we're on this subject, remember always who you are. Know it is not that others won't hurt you, they can't. You are a spirit. A holy child of God. You are free. So is everyone else.

∞

Fourth, begin today to think of me as your internal teacher. Listen to me. I'm sending you messages all the time but you don't hear me because you are seldom in a quiet enough state to hear me. I whisper. The radio and TV drown me out and you turn them on whenever you are alone. Even when the radio and TV are off, I compete with your constant internal chatter. I am always amazed at how much of your self talk -- the banter that goes on inside your mind-- is negative. No wonder you are down so much of the time.

I am always present all you need to do is simply be. All that is required is to calm your mind and to release the tensions in your muscles. I can direct you in ways you never thought possible. There are no limits to what we can co-create. The present moment is the only real time you have. The past doesn't exist and the future isn't here yet. Don't squander a precious moment. I don't mean fill each moment with activity – I mean fill each moment with an awareness of me, your internal teacher. Know the greatness within you, the power within you, and simply, calmly be.

The universe awaits to manifest your destiny. There is no lack. You don't have to wait until you get a better job, or you move, or you get a degree. All you need is within you right now. Tap into it, be still and listen to my whispers.

You have everything you need to rise to a new level of consciousness – a new level of life. You have a sacred purpose: you bring me into this family, in this area at this time to be all you are, heal whatever space you find yourself in, be happy, be free, be aware of your great power. Know God is in charge, love, be thankful for each and every moment.   And follow the whispers of me leading you to a higher life.

As I close this letter, I see your stardust is even brighter, and I know that means you are ready to start over again – to start anew. Wake up, relax, let go of the past, give others the freedom to think of you however they choose, and listen to me as I speak to you minute by minute, and through the chapters that follow and...you'll never be the same again.

Hugs,
Your Soul

2
What Are You Suppose to Be?

How do you become what you are meant to be? What are you meant to be? Why were you put on this planet? What are you suppose to accomplish? Jesus faced these same questions, and he responded, "Thy will be done", "Father, not as I would have it, but as you will". Jesus' statements are filled with confidence that God has a plan; even in the midst of chaos and confusion, in the midst of death, God has a plan for your life. There is something specific you are suppose to "be".

Why is it whenever something bad happens to us, we say, "Well, it's God's will"? Your relative dies? "It's God's will." A friend is diagnosed with cancer? "It's God's will". A natural disaster? "It's God's will". Just what kind of God is this?

We've been trained that when things happen, especially bad things, things we do not understand it's easy, and very human, to look outside of ourselves for the answer. Sometimes we fall into the trap of blaming everything and everybody. But, what if we have been interpreting the signals all wrong? What if we really believed that God's will is always for our greater good, our absolute abundance? What if we really believed the things that happen to us are part of a larger plan leading us to be what it is we are suppose to be?

The answers we seek are inside us. What you are meant to be is found within you. What then are you suppose to be?

What if God's will was that:
        You are spirit.
        You are not your body.
        You are not what you do.

What if we really believed:
        Before you were born I knew you
        (Jeremiah 1:5).
        You are made in my image and likeness
        (Genesis 1:26).
        You are gods (Psalm 82:6).

Then, consider – just consider God saying:

You reflect me. You are like me.
You are me in your world.
I am with you always.
I want to take some time to help you understand
life.
I know you want to understand.
You are always asking me "Why, Me?", you
seem to question my existence "If God really
exists, why is there evil, crime, disease, etc?"
I want to tell you.

I am God. There is no place, no situation where I
am not.
I am all, I am everywhere, I am all power. I am
everything. I am.
That's why I told Moses my name was, "I am".
The only way I work is through you.
Jesus and countless others have allowed me to
work through them.
And miracles happened.

I want you to be the same.
Yes you.

It's not as hard as it sounds.
Let's clear something up right now, I'm not talking about doing.
I don't really care what you do. As I told, Neale Donald Walsch², you are free to do whatever you choose. Which of you would ever tell your child precisely how to go out and play?
"First, swing on the swing, then the teeter-totter, then the slide". No parent does this. I don't do this.
Jesus could have been a fisherman, and it wouldn't have made any difference to me. A carpenter is what he chose – so what.
Do whatever you want to do.
You are not what you do.

"I don't work through your doing.
I work through your being."²
Your being – who you are, not what you do – was chosen before your spirit was joined to your body.
Your spirit could have chosen any spiritual attribute – any being – and it choose whatever you are currently experiencing.
It chose it, so it could reflect me.
Before he was born, Jesus' spirit chose forgiveness, that's why on the cross he said "Father, forgive them for they know not what they do." That's when he remembered who he was and why he came³.

Jesus allowed his spirit to be what it was suppose to be, and along the way miracles happened.
The greatest miracle of all happened after he uttered those words. He rose again.
I need you to "be" what your spirit has chosen to be and along the way miracles will happen.

Why? Because it is the only way for me to get involved in the experience of life.
I am all. Because of that I am scattered. Your physical body allows me to focus.
Your physical body, allows me to experience life in your world.
Your physical body allows me to heal your world.

I don't see unless it is through your eyes.
I don't hear unless you tell me.
I don't speak, unless you move your lips.
I don't touch, unless you hug.
I don't feel, unless you do.
I can't work miracles unless it is through you.

You give me a body, hands, feet, and a voice.
You give me a chance to get involved in the world I created.
I cannot be separated from you. Oh, you can ignore me. Or refuse to believe in me.
Your disbelief doesn't mean I don't exist within you – it just means I can't work through you.
I let you choose to ignore me, because I love you.
Your freedom to choose is my greatest gift to you.

*But when I can't work through you, the power to
fix, to heal, to overcome is blocked.*
*Just as when Jesus returned to Nazareth, but
could not work any miracles there.*
*The blockage on a large scale results in disease,
crime, evil.*

*You are waiting for me to solve all the problems
in the world.*
*I want to make it clear, only through you can I
solve all the problems in the world.*
You are my solution. Right now.
*You keep saying "they should do something
about that", "they should stop this", etc.*
You are the "they" – there is no one else.
There is only one way, one truth, one life to live.
Be aware of my spirit within you.
*By being aware of my spirit, you reflect me. You
can then see clearly your sacred purpose like
Jesus, and many others.*
*There is a reason you were sent to earth, at this
time, in your particular family.*
*A Course of Miracles, and Neale Donald Walsch
say it best, you were sent to heal the space.*
There is no other reason for you to be here.

You were sent to be a healer.
*Wherever you find yourself, whatever you
experience you were sent to heal, to transform.*
*You were sent to transform the ordinary into the
extraordinary.*
*You were sent so your spirit would be what it
chose to be, experience what it chose to
experience.*

That's it. That's why you're here.
You weren't sent to be a baseball player, an
actor, factory worker, or a CEO.
If you do those things--great.
But don't obsess over those "doing" activities.
That obsession will get in the way of being. And
healing will be blocked.
I am not limited by you. But the world is.

Once you complete the healing you were sent to
do, the physical body separates and the spirit
chooses again.
Another being – another healing, another
transformation.
The world is one person, one being, closer to
perfection.

Your loved ones – those who have left this
planet, no matter what the circumstances–
separated from their spirit either because they
had accomplished the healing they were sent to
accomplish, or because, their continual blocking
of the spirit made their physical body wear out.
There is no loss.
Spirit lives on. Always.

What is God's will? For you to heal the space.
For you to be what your spirit chose to be.
For you to experience who you are.
For you to be aware of the greatness within.
For you to allow me to focus my power through
you.

What then will you be?

*Will you continue to focus on doing? To be so
caught up in your doing that you've no time, or
energy left for being?
Or will you focus on being? And then all you
need to do will become clear. Miracles will
happen as you allow me to focus my power
through you.
The choice is yours. Choose miracles.*

*Be open. Listen to the spirit within.
Know that everything that happens is another
opportunity for your spirit to heal and transform.
Life is not about choosing a career – a career is
about doing.
Life is about discovering your spirit, and healing
the space.
Who are you? You are the one I am counting on.
You are it. Go within and find your being. Will
you be:
Kind.
Peaceful.
Happy.
Forgiving
Wise.
Loving.
Giving.
Honest.
Compassionate*

*That's all I need you to be. That is all I care
about.
Be just one of those, or be all, and you will
change the world.*

How? When you choose to be kind, only kind actions are appropriate.

When you choose peace, only actions that generate peace are acceptable.
When you choose to be happy, only joyfulness is tolerated.
When you choose to be wise, dumb things are not possible.
When you choose to forgive, others know they have another chance with new boundaries.
When you choose wisdom, you minister to others.
When you love without condition, you want what the other wants even if you don't think its best.
When you give, you receive.
When you have integrity, your word is your bond.
When you are compassionate, you lift up those around you.
This is how miracles happen.
Not by magic.
By choosing another way.
By being, then doing.
This is how the world will change.

What are you suppose to be? God's will is clear. Be God. Then what you need to do will be clear and every action will define precisely who you are...and you'll never be the same again.

3
Do You Have To Die to Get to Heaven?

Most of us grew up thinking heaven is the final frontier – the place you go after you die -- if you've been good. St. Peter welcomes you at the pearly gates, everyone wears white robes, has wings, and walks on clouds. Everyone is happy, kind, and peace-filled. Sound familiar?

Consider – just consider – that heaven is not the final frontier. Heaven is a state of consciousness. Heaven is now. You do not need to die to experience heaven. Heaven is wherever God is and God is within you.

Pierre Teilhard de Chardin wrote, "We are not human beings having an occasional spiritual experience, we are spirits having this particular human experience." This particular human experience may be short and illness may affect your physical body, but your spirit never dies, your spirit is always healthy. When we awaken to the spirit within, we allow God to reflect, we experience heaven on earth.

Jesus was aware of the spirit within him and allowed the reflection of God to shine. Jesus was awake to the power of God's presence within and miracles happened. Healings occurred. The hungry were fed. The sinners were loved. This is not to say "bad" things never happened. Jesus cursed. He was angry, cried, and was crucified. Through all the good times and the bad he never once forgot who he really was; a beloved child of God on a mission with a sacred purpose. Just like you.

Jesus knew everything (good, bad, neutral) happened for a purpose. The greatest gift you can give yourself is to look for the sacred purpose in everything that happens, and learn the lesson of each situation, circumstance, and experience. Miracles will happen in your life once you become aware of God's spirit is within you and allow that spirit to reflect through you in good times and bad. Miracles will happen when you awaken to the unlimited potential that is always before you even in the midst of chaos and confusion. When you awaken the spirit within, you too will heal, you will feed others, and you will love.

Heaven is a state of consciousness. And so is hell. What if these "places" are not permanent physical locations, but a constantly changing state of mind? What if God does not send us to one or the other, but we go to either at any moment by the choices we make and by how we think? How then would we live? What choices would we make?

We have a choice in the midst of chaos and confusion. We can think in terms of possibilities (heaven) or in terms of despair (hell). We can, like Jesus, after having done all we could do, choose to surrender to the sacred purpose, leave the results in God's hands, and ultimately choose heaven and be lifted up. Or we can buy in to the chaos and confusion, think we are victims, and ultimately choose hell. We can open our minds and hearts to others (heaven) or sulk in loneliness (hell). We can forgive and establish boundaries (heaven) or refuse to forgive (hell). We can share our time, talents, treasure

(heaven) or we can hoard (hell). We can choose to be
open to the spirit within (heaven) or ignore it (hell). We
can forge ahead no matter what the obstacle (heaven)
or give up (hell). Everyday, every moment we have the power to
choose thoughts of heaven or thoughts of hell. No
matter what is going on in your life, your thoughts can
make it either a heaven or a hell. You always make
the choice. Sometimes we just don't make very good
choices, we do what we think is right at the time, but
somehow it turns out like hell. Sometimes, everything
that could go wrong, does and we may find ourselves
in hell. Sometimes we find ourselves in hell and don't
know why. But when we choose to stay in the muck
and mire, we choose thoughts of hell. The good news is
that we don't have to stay there. The ability to lift
ourselves out requires thoughts of heaven. The good
news is we can always choose thoughts of heaven.

So, if heaven is not the final frontier, what does
happen when we die? If we believe only our physical
body dies and our spirit is eternal -- that must mean
our spirit lives on. What if, even in death, we have a
choice? What if we could choose to remain part of the
world, watching over our family and friends? Or, what
if we could choose not to? Or, what if we could choose
another human experience, another time, and another
place? Either way, death would lose its sting.
Perhaps, we would be more comforted when our loved
ones die. Perhaps, we would be more comfortable at
the thought of our own death.

Do you have to die to get to heaven? Just the
opposite, you have to live. Choose to be in heaven
every minute of every day. Heaven is the place you go
when you are aware of and reflect the spirit within
you. Heaven is the place where you awaken to the

unlimited possibilities that are before you. Heaven is the place where God is, and God is within you. You are a spirit having this particular human experience, and at any moment, in any circumstance, you can choose heaven.

Choose heaven, you'll experience the presence and presents of God...and you'll never be the same again.

4
What Does God Think About?

"Your thoughts are not my thoughts" says God. "As high as the heavens are above the earth, so high are my thoughts above your thoughts" (Isaiah 55:8-9).

Have you ever wondered what God thinks about? We probably assume he thinks like us. But Isaiah says God's thoughts are not our thoughts. Not only that, his thoughts are far away from ours as the heavens are from the earth. Well, just how different are our thoughts from God's?

God's thoughts are limitless - there are no boundaries to them. That means God has chosen to see in us unlimited possibility. His mind is always completely open yet how often do we choose to see only our limitations? How often do we narrow our minds, and on certain subjects close them completely?

God knows there are no accidents, everything that happens, happens for a purpose. God thinks we should march forth through each experience filled with courage, enthusiasm, expectation of great things, and not holding back. How often do we find the lesson in each moment? How often do we go through each day hoping something bad won't happen?

God knows you are more powerful than you can imagine when we choose to take action, to take a risk.

How often do we think we are powerless and procrastinate?

God knows he is a part of your life - his spirit is within you. God knows we are spirits having a human experience. How often do we think we are unworthy, unable or un-something to deserve God's presence?

God knows how to love. God loves us unconditionally. There is no small print in the contract of God's love for us. We don't have to do anything, say anything or be anything to have his love. He gives it as a free gift. How often do we love with many conditions attached, as long as you do this, or until you do that?

When faced with a choice between being right and being kind, God chooses to be kind. How often do we choose to be right, "I'll show them"?

God knows he cannot control us. God knows that it is not that we won't hurt him - but we can't hurt him. God knows he is free to feel anyway he chooses to feel. He owns his feelings - no one can make him feel any particular feeling. How often do we think others make us feel sad, lonely, hurt, or happy? How often do we think we can control others? How often do we try to hold on to people, restrict and limit them? God knows this is not healthy. God knows that by letting go others can grow.

Isaiah's words now make a lot of sense, don't they? God's thoughts are higher than our thoughts. Fortunately, we have the power to change our thoughts. The greatest gift you have been given, the source of your power, the hope for your future is the gift of choice. The power to choose your thoughts, the ability to see things differently separates us from the animal kingdom. You have the power - the responsibility - to think differently.

John the Baptist said "Repent." St. Paul told us, "You will be transformed by the renewal of your mind". Both are saying the same thing. Change your mind. Change your life. Think like God:

∞ Find the lesson in each moment.

∞ March forth through each moment filled with enthusiasm, courage, and expectation, giving it all you have.

∞ Know that God's spirit is within you guiding you to your unlimited potential.

∞ Give the gift of unconditional love freely - never take it back – allow others the freedom to walk away from your love and that is okay - the gift remains.

∞ Choose to be kind - being right elevates only you - being kind lifts up everyone.

∞ Know it is not that others won't hurt you, but they can't hurt you. The slings and stones of others do not diminish us.

∞ Own your feelings, know that another can never make you feel happy or sad.

∞ Give others freedom to feel about you anyway they choose. Let go of trying to control and manipulate others.

∞ Know your life has a sacred purpose - there is a reason you are on this planet.

∞ Be all that you are and leave the results in God's hands.

Think like God and your thoughts will change. When you change your thoughts, your life will change...and you'll never be the same again.

5
Where Is The Kingdom?

What comes to mind when you think of a kingdom? A huge castle, servants, wealth, a king, a queen, jewels, food. In short, extravagance. An outlandish display of great wealth. And if you go beyond the material aspect, you think of strength, courage, and power.

What comes to mind when you think of Jesus' words "The Kingdom of God is within you?" Consider - just consider – Jesus meant all the wealth God has is in you. You are the jewels of God. You are the castle of God. In you are all the riches, strength, courage, and power of God.

Are you thinking, oh no, not me, I'm not worthy? Understand this, if you are still breathing, you are worthy. Les Brown, often says "I know something about you and I don't even know you - you have more going for you than you can ever imagine, you are more powerful than you know - you have greatness within you"[4].

What is this greatness? It is the kingdom of God within you. Through you God can do great things, but to accomplish these things, you first may have to go through some tough times. These tough times give you the skills to proceed to the next level of your life, the next step in your evolution, the higher consciousness.

Positive and negative events and circumstances happen to you all the time. In the midst of the negative, most people give up. Most people stop believing. Most people ignore the kingdom within and seek it outside of themselves, and are filled with despair. Most refuse to consider that there is a lesson in the event or circumstance.

Others march onward knowing all the power, strength, and courage of the kingdom is available to meet, rise above, and overcome any obstacle. These people will succeed because they know the power of the kingdom of God is within.

Let this sink in a moment. God is in you. Right now and at every moment. You can never separate yourself from God. You are God's messenger. You are a holy child of God. You are spirit. God is not outside of you in heaven or somewhere -- anywhere. You now know exactly where God is and what God looks like. God is in you. God looks like you.

What if you start to believe this? What would your life be like? Jesus believed beyond a shadow of doubt that the kingdom of God was in him. He didn't wish it, hope for it.   He didn't think he had to earn it, nor did he think he was un-worthy.   He knew it, believed it, he felt it.   Because of this he loved unconditionally, forgave, healed, fed the hungry, taught. Also he suffered.   But in his suffering, he showed us it is possible to rise above our pain and sorrow. He showed us how to live. He showed us what our lives would be like once we believed the kingdom of God is within us.

What if we believed God loves us so much he wanted to give us something, but couldn't decide what to give us - so he gave us the entire kingdom? He held nothing back. He gave us all he had. How many times have you given a gift to someone, but never saw the

person use your gift? Didn't it make you wonder why
you bothered giving it?

Use the gifts God has given you. Embrace who
you are -- the good, the not so good. David
Augsburger wrote, "I change not when I am attempting
to be what I am not, but when I am owning what,
where, who I truly am. Then I am free to grow"[5].

Own and embrace what, where, and who you
truly are. Move through sadness, sorrow, worry, fear,
impatience, anger, jealousy, and envy – then you will
be free to grow. In the face of challenges and obstacles,
know there is a valid reason for everything that
happens, and know these challenges and obstacles
make you stronger and lead you to your greatness.

Begin today to awaken the kingdom of God
within you:

∞ Lift up another - knowing that when you lift
up another, you also rise.

∞ Give to others unceasingly - knowing that
you receive only what you give.

∞ Be patient and kind in every moment –
especially to yourself, knowing that you are
a reflection of God and without your
reflection God is invisible.

∞ Create time in your day to open your mind
to the peace and joy of the kingdom.

∞ Know you are free of all limits - you are in
the kingdom where all things are possible.

∞ Own, embrace and move through all sadness, sense of loss, anxiety, and fears so you can grow.

∞ Align your priorities with those of the kingdom - God first, you second, others third.

∞ Live as Jesus did, knowing that the kingdom – and all its power, strength, courage, and riches – is within you.

Where is the Kingdom? The kingdom of God is within you, avail yourself of all its riches, power, courage...and you'll never be the same again.

6
What Are You Waiting For?

In Matthew 28:20, Jesus' last words were "Know that I am with you always." Would you agree that "always" means right now, every day, every hour, every minute and every second? If so, then can you agree with the saying "Wherever you are, God is"?

How aware are you that God is present in your life every second? Each second that goes by without your awareness of God is time wasted. Each second you are aware of God's presence is timeless. If you believe God is present in your life every second – offering you all you need, all the riches of the kingdom – don't you think that maybe, your life would be different?

Maybe you might stand a little taller, smile a bit more, be a bit more enthusiastic, kinder, patient, and worry less. You might be positive, let go of negative feelings and emotions, and be free of loneliness. Try as you might you cannot separate yourself from God. Even if you don't believe in him, he is with you always. Even if you don't want him, he is with you always. How long will you continue to ignore your greatest ally, your power, and your unlimited potential? How long will you fight against the universe? How long will you stay stuck? Why wait anymore?

What does the Second Coming of Jesus mean to you? Some future event? Something you'll have to die to experience? Some cataclysmic earth shaking phenomenon?

Open your mind and consider – just consider – another meaning, another interpretation to the Second Coming.

What if the Second Coming of Jesus happens every moment you realize that wherever you are, God is. Every second God is present within you.

Every second, God needs your voice to be heard. Every second, God needs your hands to reach out to others. Every second, God needs your feet to take him to others, needs your heart to show his great love, needs your laughter to show his joy. God needs your calmness to bring peace.

There is a reason you are on this planet, in this time, in this church, in this city, in this family. That reason is, you have a message to deliver. You have a sacred purpose.

Without you there is no Second Coming of Jesus. You are the Second Coming. The Second Coming happens when you wake up and realize that every second, every moment of your life, you reflect God to all you encounter and there are no limits to what you can accomplish.

Do you realize just how special you are, how important you are, how blessed? Right now and every second, your family needs you, your church needs you, and your universe needs you. God's work is incomplete without your participation.

What are you waiting for? There is no time to delay. Begin now, start over now. Reach out to someone today. Show kindness today. Lift up another today. Quiet your inner and outer world so you can hear the voice of God and allow his reflection to shine through. Know that wherever you are, God is...and you'll never be the same again.

7
Are You Happy?

What if happiness is your function, your purpose in the world? What if the reason you are on the planet is to be happy, right now, this minute – no matter what?

Jesus (John 10:10) said, "I came that you might have life and have it to the full". Some translations say, "I came that you might have joy and have it abundantly".

Jesus was not referring to sometime in the future, but right now. God wants us to be happy and Jesus came to show us how. Jesus showed us a life filled with God's presence is a life of miracles. Jesus showed us how to be happy. And oh yes, there will be trials and tribulations, but Jesus showed us it is possible to rise above them.

Think about the best day you've ever had, remember the feelings, the joy, the happiness? Jesus came to show us how everyday could be just like that. How many of those best days can you think of? Just one or two in your whole life? What has happened to us? How did we stray so far from this basic spiritual principle? Why aren't our days filled with abundant joy?

What has happened is that, for whatever reason, we started to believe that happiness comes from outside us. We started to believe we needed some event, circumstance or person to make us happy. Truth is, no event, no circumstance, no job, no person, nor any amount of money can make you happy.

Why aren't we happy every moment? Why don't our faces beam smiles all day long? Because we forget – happiness comes from within. Father John Powell suggests the placement of a sign on your bathroom mirror (where you will see it every morning) which reads: "You are looking at the face of the person who is responsible for your happiness today![6]"

Consider – just consider – what you would be like if you believed your function, your purpose in the world is to be happy:

∞ You know only you are responsible for your happiness.

∞ You know that happiness is a choice.

∞ You smile often.

∞ You find joy in every moment.

∞ You cherish laughter.

∞ You feel God's presence within, guiding and directing you to your absolute abundance and good.

∞ You trust that there is a valid reason for everything that happens.

∞ You seek out the lesson in every experience.

∞ You embrace yourself just as you are.

∞ You find in your sorrow and pain the power,
   strength and courage to rise again.

Are you happy? Jesus came so that you might
have joy and have it abundantly. This means that
happiness is your function, your purpose in the world.
Happiness is possible today, this minute, not when
you are older, or thinner, not when you move, not
when you make a million dollars, not when you die.
Happiness is possible when you know that God is
within.

Believe that the reason you are on the planet is
to be happy...and you'll never be the same again.

8
How Do You Love?

Jesuit Father John Powell, wrote, "Love is either conditional or unconditional - there is no other possibility. Either I attach conditions to my love or I do not. To the extent that I do attach such conditions to my love, I do not really love you."[7] Similarly, Guy Lynch says, "Absolute love has no conditions."[8]

In Jesus' time, a pan scale was the tool of measurement. The store proprietor put a known weight equal to the weight of what the customer wanted to buy on one side of the scale. He'd fill the other with whatever was being purchased. When the two scales were equal it was done. Nowadays, we don't use pan scales except when we love. "You do this for me - and then I do this for you" - Sound familiar? This is conditional love, one act weighed against the other.

Fr. John Powell defines conditional love as an exchange that says I love you as long as or until. As long as you never lie to me, as long as I get what I want out of this relationship. Conditional love says if you stop doing this - I stop. If you don't call me - I won't call you. If you forget to send me a card on my birthday – I'll forget yours. If I don't get a Holiday card from you, I'll take you off my list. Pan scale love isn't real love.

Only unconditional love is real love. Fr. Powell says unconditional – that is, true love, is always a gift, not an exchange. It means going all out all the time-- not just 50% but 150%. Unconditional love has no pan scales. Unconditional love means there are no conditions or strings attached. You don't have to do anything, say anything, or be anything. There is no small print in the contract. Unconditional love says I am giving you a gift; the gift of my love and I'll never take it back. It is yours. My love for you is not conditioned on your response. You can't earn it. I choose to give it to you.

Unconditional love is the way Jesus loved all with whom he came into contact. Jesus had no need of pan scales. He chose to love his disciples even though they didn't get his message, even though they deserted him. He loved the disciples without expectation of a response. He proved it is not what we get out of a relationship that is important, it is what we give. He gave the gift of his love to all he encountered and kept on giving it.

The good news is, God loves us the same way. We don't earn God's love, we don't deserve it, we don't win it. God gives us the gift of his unconditional love. His love is a free gift with no strings attached, no rules to follow, no obligations to keep.

How do you learn to love unconditionally? You start by loving God unconditionally. No matter the circumstances, remember who God is and who you are. Love God without conditions not because he needs your love. But because it is who you are.

We've all spent the greater part of our lives loving God conditionally. How many times have we said, "God if you just get me out of this particular jam - I'll go to church every Sunday?". When we are in trouble, we get out the pan scales and begin to barter for God's love.

Bartering doesn't work because God couldn't possibly love us more. In fact, there is nothing we could do that would make him love us more or less. God gives us the gift of his unconditional love. It is not conditioned on our response. We have it whether we want it, think we need it, or don't believe it.

After you learn to love God unconditionally, start to love yourself unconditionally too. Now is the time to make your self-talk positive, nurturing, and supportive, instead of negative, badgering, and relentless. Let a new era of unconditional love begin. Stop battering yourself with your failures and reminding yourself of your shortcomings. It is ok to make a mistake. It is ok to make a lot of mistakes. You are not condemned. God forgives the worst thing you've ever done. Forgive yourself. Love yourself without conditions and you'll find negative habits and behaviors will no longer be acceptable, because you love yourself way too much.

Finally, start to love others without conditions. Can you imagine what your relationships would be if based on the foundation of unconditional love; a love freely given, not conditioned on a response. Imagine a relationship that says I give you wings to fly, not chains to be tied down. Imagine a relationship that hopes for the best in all your endeavors; a relationship which says you have my support always, I freely give you my greatest gift and there are no strings attached to it.

But please remember, unconditional love does not give license to someone to walk all over you. You are not a doormat. Unconditional love says, I love God first, then myself and I love myself so much I will not tolerate any abuse. Unconditional love says I recognize even though I've given you the gift of my love, you have chosen not to reciprocate it, and that is fine. You'll always have my gift, but I move on. I let you go.

Unconditional love is not new. Jesus displayed it. St. Paul defined it (1 Corinthians 13:47): "Love is patient; love is kind. Love is not jealous, it does not put on airs, it is not snobbish. Love is never rude, it is not self-seeking, it is not prone to anger; neither does it brood over injuries. Love does not rejoice in what is wrong but rejoices with the truth. There is no limit to love's forbearance, to its trust, its hope, its power to endure."

Let's transform it. You love unconditionally when:

∞ You choose to be patient.

∞ You choose to be kind at all times.

∞ You don't lift yourself up without lifting up all those around you.

∞ You don't seek what you get but focus on what you give.

∞ You are prone to compassion.

∞ You let go of pan scale conditional love and give love as a free gift with no strings attached.

∞ You forgive and set proper boundaries so you do not become a doormat. You don't cling. You let go.

∞ You know your love is more powerful than rejection, more powerful than death – there is no limit to it.

When you love unconditionally you are free of all limits, and love is no longer a pan scale experience. You are full of patience, trust, hope and have the power to endure all things knowing you are not alone.

How do you love? There is only one way. Love unconditionally not because others need it, because it is who you are...and you'll never be the same again.

9
Where Is the Glory?

Have you read the Bible cover to cover? Many people have a hard time with it because the stories are a bit obtuse. Written so long ago, in a different culture it is often hard to understand the stories. But, oh those stories. There are murders, wars, pestilence, plagues, and deceit. There is also much glory. But often, the glory is buried beneath negative circumstances. The real message is often lost in a mire of cultural differences or inadequate translations.

There's no question a lot of bad things happened. Adam and Eve were thrown out of the garden of Eden; Lot's wife was turned into a salt pillar; a flood destroyed all but Noah and the Ark; and Jesus was crucified. If we dwell on these bad things, we miss the glory.

We have focused on the bad things too long. So much so we think that all we can expect is bad things on earth and joy only in heaven. The good news is that in every negative story there is a positive message for us - a message of choice, a message of listening, and a message for life.

Every Bible Story has a powerful purpose. The power of the message is visible only when we focus on the glory. The message is simple. We are free to choose to be in or out of God's presence. We are free to choose to listen to God or not. Adam and Eve chose to be out. All of Noah's neighbors and Lot's wife chose not to listen.

All of the stories of the Bible are about one thing; when we do not follow the voice of God within us, but look for something outside of us to guide us, we get in trouble. Adam and Eve choose to listen to the snake, and they lost paradise. Noah's neighbors refused to listen to the warnings and they drowned. Lot's wife when clearly instructed not to look back, did so and became a pillar of salt.

God has a plan for us, a plan for our glory, for our abundance and our good. But, the success of the plan is up to us. God knew paradise was better, but Adam and Eve chose otherwise. God knew a boat was required, but only Noah built one. God knew what was best, but they freely chose otherwise. The glory of the story is that God allowed them to make the mistakes. He didn't force them to obey. Every Bible story has a similar theme.

God speaks, people listen, people choose. When people choose the opposite way – opposite of what God says – death is the result. And then there is the story of Jesus' life. He listened and chose to follow. But wait a minute, he died too. What is going on?

God wanted Jesus' life to show us the way to live. He wanted us to know that while we may suffer and die, we will rise, that suffering and pain can never conquer the spirit which dwells within us. The suffering and pain is limited only to our physical bodies. Our spirit is always healed and whole. No matter how negative, there is a plan, a purpose and as long as we don't give up, we will understand it. There is a better way to live.

Jesus' day-to-day life shows us the way, but sometimes we lose sight of it because we focus so heavily on his suffering and pain. Aren't you tired of focusing on the suffering and the pain? Let's focus on the glory. Let's be lifted up.

You are probably familiar with the Good Friday Way of the Cross – 14 painful, suffering stations along Jesus route to the crucifixion. Consider – just consider – a story of glory. A Good Friday "Way of the Resurrection" with joyful, empowering stations along Jesus' life that give us courage and strength to make it through the storms of our own life.

The 1st Station of the Way of the Resurrection: Jesus Gives Peace.

Peace begins inside of you. Quiet your mind, relax your muscles. You are peace.

The 2nd Station of the Way of the Resurrection: Jesus Calls God "Abba".

Abba is Aramaic for 'papa' or dad. You are so close, that you can call God whatever you need him to be, dad, mom, mama. You call God "Abba".

The 3rd Station of the Way of the Resurrection: Jesus Says Do Not Be Afraid.

Move beyond fear. Transform the energy contained in your fear to face your challenges. Take advantage of the energy in your fear and use it to overcome all obstacles. You are not afraid of being afraid.

The 4th Station of the Way of the Resurrection: Jesus Loves Unconditionally.

There are no conditions to God's love, no strings attached, no fine print in the contract. God is giving you a gift, a gift of his unconditional love and he'll

never take it back. You are loved.   You love
unconditionally.

The 5th Station of the Way of the Resurrection: Jesus
Teaches.
        By his teaching, his example, his words, Jesus
showed us how to be awake to the spirit within. You
are awake. You teach.

The 6th Station of the Way of the Resurrection: Jesus
Forgives.
        God forgives us. Your challenge is to forgive
yourself. Then to establish boundaries, forgive others,
and let them go. You forgive.

The 7th Station of the Way of the Resurrection: Jesus
Prays.
        Jesus re-energizes his spirit, by listening to the
power within. When you calm your inner and outer
world, you'll hear the quiet voice of God within. You
pray.

The 8th Station of the Way of the Resurrection: Jesus
Asks Us To Believe.
        Know - truly know - God is in you and expect
miracles to happen. You believe.

The 9th Station of the Way of the Resurrection: Jesus
Nurtures and Heals.
        Jesus showed compassion. Compassion is not
to take pity but to extend care to others because you
see their need.[5b] You are compassion.

The 10th Station of the Way of the Resurrection: Jesus Directs .

Jesus clearly stated what you are to do, "your business is to follow me". And when you follow, you "will do the works Jesus did, and far greater than these" (John 14:12). Your direction is clear, you have unlimited potential.

The 11th Station of the Way of the Resurrection: Jesus Practices Non-Judgment.

"If you want to avoid judgment, stop passing judgement" (Matthew 7:1). Today you judge nothing that occurs. You practice non-judgment.

The 12th Station of the Way of the Resurrection: Jesus Gives Thanks.

Prior to feeding 4000 people with seven loaves and a few small fish, Jesus gave thanks. The food multiplied so that seven hampers were filled with leftovers. Giving constant thanks multiplies your talents and increases your potential. With an attitude of gratitude, nothing is impossible. You give thanks.

The 13th Station of the Way of the Resurrection: Jesus Surrenders.

After having done all he could do, Jesus left the results in God's hands and let go. Once you do all that you can, leave the results in God's hands, and trust that a greater plan will unfold. You surrender.

The 14th Station of the Way of the Resurrection: Jesus Rises Up.

Each time the path you are on takes an unexpected turn, trust there is a sacred plan. Each time you fail, know we can start over. Each time thoughts of lack and limitation enter your mind, remember your unlimited potential. Trust that everything that happens to us, happens for a reason; when you start over, when you free your mind of limiting thoughts; you are lifted up. When you are lifted up, all rise. You rise.

Where is the glory? Within you. Choose to be in God's presence, choose to listen to the voice within you. It's the only way to stay in paradise, to keep afloat in the turbulence of life, to become un-stuck in the ruts of life, and to rise up.

The glory is more powerful than the pain. The resurrection is more powerful than the crucifixion. Glory attracts glory. Heed the spirit within, and a life of glory will be attracted to you like a magnet...and you'll never be the same again.

10
How Comfortable Are You?

"The Lord said to Abram, go forth from the land of your kinsfolk and from your fathers house to a land that I will show you. I will make of you a great nation, I will bless you, I will make your name great so that you will be a blessing to others (Genesis 12:1-3)."

I know you have heard this story a million times but consider the glory of this story as personalized by Les Brown. Imagine God saying this to you right now: "I want to make you a great person. I want you to be more than ordinary. I want you to be prosperous, happy, holy. You will be a source of prosperity, happiness, and holiness to others. Who wouldn't say yes to this? Of course, we all want this. Then, God says, *'Before I can make you a great person, you have to do something'*. What is it? God responds, *'You have to leave your kinsfolk and your father's house and go to a land I will show you'*. Do you still want this?"⁹ Of course you do, because it is the only way to achieve all the greatness that God has in store for you.

God's message to Abram was there are plans for you - plans to make you great - but you need to do something. First you have to leave your comfort zone, take some chances, take some risks. Second, you have to leave your kinsfolk. Sometimes family and friends may not be good for you. Sometimes as Les Brown says they may be toxic or energy draining. You don't need toxic people who beat you physically, or mentally through constant criticism or negativism. You will become great when you leave these energy draining people. Third, trust that God will show you where to go and who you need in your life. These will be people who will affirm you, who lift you up, and who will believe in you.

Les Brown often asks, "Why is it that most people don't achieve their greatness in life? Because they are satisfied. They are comfortable, average and ordinary. If you want to achieve your greatness, you have to get out of your comfort zone and you have to leave people who aren't good for you."[8]

Think about an eagle's nest. The mother eagle knows that her babies will be great birds. But first, they have to leave the nest. The babies don't want to go. They are very cozy and comfortable. But not great. Great is soaring through the air. The baby eagles don't know it, they don't know the power within them. So, sometimes the mother eagle has to kick them out of the nest in order for them to stretch their wings and fly - in order for them to achieve their greatness.

What are the cozy, comfortable nests of your life? What comfort zone is holding you back, keeping you from experiencing the power you have within? How do you become great? How do you become a blessing to others? By trusting in God. Trusting enough to step out of your comfort zone. Trusting you'll be encouraged by people around you, who love you and want the best for you, by people who see in you the greatness God sees. Trusting that when you step out of your comfort zone, though you don't know where you are going, earthly angels will be there to help you or to pick you up should you stumble. Trusting that God knows what he is doing and knows where you are headed. You are headed to your greatness.

How comfortable are you? So comfortable that you've become average and ordinary? Be like Abram;

go forth from your comfort zone, leave toxic people
behind, trust in God, and you will be what God wants
you to be – great, extraordinary, blessed, and a
blessing to others...and you'll never be the same again.

11
What Are You Going to Do About It?

In the Gospel According to Matthew (5:1-12), Matthew writes: "When he saw the crowds he went up on the mountainside. He began to teach them, 'How blest are the poor in spirit: the reign of God is theirs. Blest too are the sorrowing: they shall be consoled. Blest are the lowly: they shall inherit the land. Blest are they who hunger and thirst for holiness: they shall have their fill. Blest are they who show mercy: mercy shall be theirs. Blest are the single hearted for they shall see God. Blest are the peacemakers: they shall be called sons of God. Blest are those persecuted for holiness' sake: the reign of God is theirs. Blest are you when they insult you and persecute you and utter every kind of slander against you because of me. Be glad and rejoice, for your reward is great in heaven.' "

The Sermon on the Mount was Jesus' first sermon. It was the first time Jesus addressed a crowd and the very first words out of his mouth were "Blessed are you". His first talk took place on a mountain talking about the mountain of problems people have. For each problem he gave a solution. Each solution required the people to do something. Action was required. It still is.

He could have said a lot of things in his first sermon. He could have pointed out their sinfulness, their weakness but he did not. This was probably the first time the people did not hear about how sinful they were, how many laws they had broken, how they could, should, must follow the rules better. They must have been shocked and relieved to hear, perhaps for the first time, you are blessed. You are ok. No matter what you have done, no matter what is going on in your life, you are blessed. He chose to lift them up not to beat them down. He chose to talk about their greatness not their weakness. He chose to speak to them where they were - not about a future place. He chose to fill them with hope not create despair.

Jesus knew their sufferings and lifted them up. Jesus gave the people on that mountain the first glimpse of the meaning of the resurrection. He told them, it's possible to rise above sorrow, lowliness, hunger. These have no power over you when you choose to show mercy, bring peace, bring God's love.

Webster defines "blessed" as "eternal bliss". Are you enjoying eternal bliss? Right now, this minute? Eternal bliss doesn't mean there won't be sadness -- crucifixions and pain -- but it does mean we have the power to rise above them. This power is the presence of God in our lives.

Consider – just consider – the Sermon on the Mount given today:

∞ You enjoy eternal bliss when: you know you are a spirit, free of all limitations, aware of all riches of the kingdom that God is waiting to give to you.

∞ You enjoy eternal bliss when: you lift yourself out of the depths of sorrow, depression, despair, and addiction; and feel God's strength is always present within you.

∞ You enjoy eternal bliss when: in the midst of your suffering you still feel God's power and presence; and when you are aware of God's compassion for you.

∞ You enjoy eternal bliss when: you recognize your low self-esteem, and choose to change your mind and change your life and be lifted up to a higher level of consciousness.

∞ You enjoy eternal bliss when: you deliver unspoken, unknown, random acts of kindness and giving because it is who you are.

∞ You enjoy eternal bliss when: you forgive; as you forgive so will you be forgiven.

∞ You enjoy eternal bliss when: you believe God is present and within you every moment of every day.

∞ You enjoy eternal bliss when: you bring God's peace to every circumstance, thought, event or moment by remembering who God is and who you are.

∞ You enjoy eternal bliss when: you stop persecuting yourself with doubt, fear, worry and anxiety and relish the freedom God gives.

∞ You enjoy eternal bliss when: you are happy and rejoice - for you are blessed and there is no end to the blessings you will receive because the kingdom is within you.

The Sermon on the Mount taught that the way to achieve eternal bliss is by taking action. Taking action is the way to happiness. Taking action can move mountains of doubt and fear and it can fill valleys of despair with hope. Taking action was required 2000 years ago and it is required today.

When you think you are in hell and faced with poverty, sorrow, lowliness, hunger, thirst - decide what you are going to do about it and take action. So, the question is What Are You Going to Do About It? Jesus' answer, in his first sermon, was remember you are here to enjoy eternal bliss. Take any action required to achieve it.

Choose to rise above the circumstances that may be negative and limiting. Choose to take action toward freedom. Live the Sermon on the Mount and you'll always know exactly what to do. You'll discover that not only are you able to rise above any obstacle, but you'll lift others up along the way. Once you begin this journey there will be no mountain too high and no valley too low to keep you from enjoying eternal bliss. You are blessed.

What are you going to do about it? You are going to remember why you are here and you will conquer that mountain, and fill that valley.... and you'll never be the same again.

12
Will You Say Yes to the Questions of Life?

In the Gospel According to John, Jesus asks a lot of questions. He always gave those close to him the opportunity to make a choice. The choice is always between God and whatever else is in the way. The response required is either a "yes" or a "no" to God. If the answer is yes, miracles happen.

At the wedding of Cana, Jesus' mother tells him "They have no more wine" (John 2:3), Jesus asks her, "Woman how does this concern of yours involve me?" (John 2:4) Everyone is free to say "yes" or "no", even Jesus. He chose to say "yes", and a miracle happened, he turned ordinary water turned into fine wine.

Jesus asks Nicodemus (John 3:9), "You still do not understand?" How long will you choose to ignore your greatest teacher?

He asks his disciples (John 6:61), "Does it shake your faith?" Does the idea of being one with me scare you so much you will deny it? Or, will you choose to believe?

Later he asks them (John 7:67), "Do you want to leave me too?" And (John 7:70), "Did I not chose you myself?" Jesus re-affirmed his love without requiring the disciples to earn it.

At the Last Supper, Jesus asks his disciples (John 16:31), "Do you really believe?"

He questions Pilate (John 18:34), "Are you saying this on your own or have others been telling you about me?"

After his resurrection Jesus asks Mary Magdalene (John 20:15), "Woman, why are you

weeping? Who is it you are looking for?" He asks
Peter, James, and John – all of whom have gone back
to being fisherman (John 21:5), "Children, have you
caught anything to eat?" He asks Peter (John 21:15),
"Do you love me?" And, finally, when the disciples
question the future, he asks, as he asked his mother
(John 21:22), "How does that concern you?"

What if, the questions Jesus asked 2000 years
ago are the same questions he asks of us today?
Jesus showed us miracles happen when we say "yes"
to God. Jesus spent his time on earth giving all who
knew him, met him, interacted with him the power to
choose a "yes" or a "no" to God. He did not treat
people like robots - he always asked them the
questions of life. They were free to choose God or not.
So are we.

Consider – just consider – your answers to
these same questions of life:

Jesus asked his Mother, "How does this concern of
yours involve me?"

Believe God is part of each of your concerns, if
you believe that now is the moment to take action,
miracles will happen and the water of your life will
turn into fine wine.

"Do you still not understand?"

If the Nicodemus in you still doesn't
understand, choose to spend time reading, learning,
more and more from the spiritual writers of today?

"Does it shake your faith?"

Does the Peter in you allow your faith to be
shaken in sickness, death, or loss of a job? Or, like

Jesus, will you meet, move through, and rise above all obstacles?

"Do you want to leave me too?"
Does the Judas in you, choose to walk away from God's presence, to ignore the spirit within, to pretend you don't need God? Or will you choose to be awake and aware of the presence and power of God within you?

"Did I not choose you myself?"
Will you choose to remember God loves you unconditionally and you do not earn his love nor can you lose it? You are free to remember or ignore it.

"Do you really believe?"
Will you choose to believe that God is not outside of you, but within?

"Are you saying this on your own or have others been telling you about me?"
Will the Pilate in you choose to give up your power and allow others to make your choices for you? Or, regardless of peer pressure, will you stand firm and choose God always.

"Why are you weeping - Who is it you are looking for"?
Will you choose to believe that everything happens for a sacred purpose and what you are looking   for   is   within   you?

"Have you caught anything to eat?"
    Will the fisherman in you cast the net according to the voice of God within? If you say "yes", trust in God, move out of your comfort zone, then you will know which direction to cast your net and find it overflowing with abundance. It will overflow with the courage, power, and strength you need to move forward.

"Do you love me?"
    Will you choose to love unconditionally at all times? Will you choose to be kind to each person you meet? Will you establish the proper priority of life, God first, you second, others third?

"How does that concern you?"
    Will you do all you can do and let the results be in God's hands?

    The questions Jesus asked his followers 2000 years ago are being asked of you today. Each minute, each hour, each day. Say "yes" to the questions of life, choose God, expect miracles to happen...and you'll never be the same again.

13
What Are You Going to Get?

Have you ever pondered the question, "What's in it for me?" If I do x, y, or z, what will I get? Will I get a little or a lot?

Perhaps you've heard others say, "I stopped going to church because I just wasn't getting anything out of it?" Or, "I stopped calling Mrs. Smith because she did all the talking." Or, "I stopped working so hard, because my boss did not appreciate me or promote me."

We make these kinds of limiting decisions all day long. We aren't getting what we think we should, or what we think we deserve and we decide to withdraw, to hide our light under a bushel. We decide it is just not worth adding any flavor to our days. Days turn into weeks, weeks into months, months into years and before you know it, life becomes pretty dark, dull, and boring.

Consider – just consider – the possibility that the real question is "What Do I Bring?" not "What Am I Going To Get?" What is it that I bring to this church, this relationship, this job? All of our lives we've been on the take. Yet, no matter how much we get we still feel empty. So we try to get more. In a frenzy to get more and more, trying to make sure we come out on top, we lose sight of what we bring.

We need to put things in perspective, come to terms with the reason we are on this planet in this time, at this time. Why are you here? Jesus simply says because "You are the salt of the earth". All who cook know that without salt food is bland, dull, boring.

Oh it is edible, but it is barely worth eating. So Jesus is saying, you are here because without your spirit, life is dull, bland, and boring.   Oh, it is tolerable, but barely worth living.

Salt adds zest to food. If you are the salt of the earth, you add zest to life. You bring to life full flavor. It is what you bring not what you get that makes life meaningful and exciting.   Your spirit is destined to bring energy, zest, and enthusiasm. Your spirit is destined to bring integrity, kindness, laughter, unconditional love, wisdom, support, fairness, etc. You may bring to life all of these, just a couple, or maybe just one.

When Jesus was tempted in the desert - the temptations were about getting – and he showed us how to handle them. "Look", the ego said, "you can get bread" – Jesus responded "I am the bread of life." "Look, you can get the help of angels" – Jesus responded, I am an angel".   "Look, you can get a kingdom" – Jesus responded "The kingdom of God is within me". Jesus knew and wanted to show us that things outside us, really don't help us. The things outside of us are about getting. It is the things inside us that matter and what is inside of us, we need to bring forth.

Life is not about getting. All we need is within us. Life is about bringing forth the spirit within. Jesus knew his gift was to show that God was within him, and so within each of us. We don't "get" God. We "bring" him to life.

What will you bring forth today? Will you bring forth your full flavor or, will you be flat, dull and boring? Will you let your light shine or hide it under a bushel?

Will you expect a smile or bring one? Will you hope someone helps you or will you give a hand to someone? Will you wait for a kind word or speak kindly to someone?   When you bring these simple actions (and countless others) to the table of life, instead of waiting to get them, miracles will happen. There will be too many flavors for life to be dull, too much light to be hid under a bushel.

What are you going to get?   Only what you bring. Without the spirit you bring to this planet, this church, this relationship, this job, life is dark, dull and boring. But when you bring forth the gifts your spirit has to share, your life will glow and be full of flavor ... and you'll never be the same again.

14
How Busy Are You?

Two thousand years ago, in Bethlehem, Jesus was born in a stable. At the time of Jesus' birth, the world sent a strong signal, there is no space for God, we are too busy. Not much has changed in 2000 years. In fact, we are sending those same signals today.

Our lives are complicated, relationships require a lot of work and time. The kids need to be shuttled from one activity--soccer, dancing, basketball, football, piano--to another. Work invented a thing called casual overtime, an extra 1-2 hours a day without pay. Then there are the chores -- the cleaning, laundry, grocery shopping. So much to do and so little time. Every moment is full. We are too busy.

The question is, "Is there room in your busy life for God" Probably not. Do you need to make room for God? Yes, if you want miracles to happen.

The reason Joseph and Mary had to go to Bethlehem was because Caesar ordered a worldwide census. Perhaps, now is a good time for us to take a census too - a personal inventory of where God is in your life - right now. What do you spend most of your thoughts on? What do you make plans for? How do you spend your quiet moments, if you have any quiet moments?

Did you answer "God" to any of the three questions? Are most of your thoughts of God? Do your plans revolve around God? Do you spend quiet moments with God?

The good news is that God is within you. The bad news is that we choose to ignore him. We have within us the greatest power but, we allow our lives to be cluttered with everything but God. We seldom draw on our greatest strength, God. We think we are alone. We think we have to fix everything, do everything, and create everything by ourselves. We get so caught up in "doing" we lose sight of "being". And our "being" is the most important part of our life – it is the God part.

Let's get our priorities in the right order. The stuff we do is not who we are. We need to focus on our "being" – what kind of person we want to "be" not what we want to "do". Again, our proper priorities are God first, me second, others third.

Jesus said with regret, "Many are called, few are chosen". Consider – just consider – this means everyone has God within, but few choose to clear out the clutter, create a space to be open, listen, and change. In the Bible stories, God always talked to the prophets or he sent angels to tell people what to do. It seems strange that God who has communicated with us for thousands of years would suddenly stop. Guess what? He hasn't stopped. We have just stopped listening. We are so caught up in our "doing" we no longer are aware of his presence. We are so busy, we don't create a space to hear God's voice. We just need to make room and start listening.

How do you make room for God? You need to establish boundaries and let go of some "busy-ness" that fills up every open space in your life. You may have to do some weeding in the garden of your life. What is it you can do to make room for and pay attention to the inner voice of God? Try following the advice of Walt Disney.

Late in his life Walt Disney was asked to share his ingredients for success. He said "There are four essential ingredients: think, believe, dream and dare." [10]

To successfully create a space for God in your life, follow these same four principles:

THINK

Think about the busy-ness cluttering the garden of your life and weed it out. Think about what "doing" you need to let go of so you can "be". Think about and re-discover who you are meant to "be".

BELIEVE

Believe God is sending messages to you all day long. These messages are for your good, they direct you, save you, help you each moment. Believe that with God all things are possible. Believe that sometimes God communicates directly and you'll hear an inner voice. Sometimes he sends "angels" to get your attention and direct you. These angels may be friends, relatives, ministers, strangers, billboards, movies, book titles, magazine articles, Walt Disney.

DREAM

Dream about your sacred purpose. Create a vision for what will happen when your "being" is more important than your "doing". Dream about the abundance God has in store for you. Dream about the blessings that await you. Dream about how your prosperity will lift up others. Dream big!

DARE

Dare to trust that once you awaken to the spirit within and determine what you want to "be", what you need to "do" will become very clear.   Be open, listen and dare to move on the path that has been cleared for you.   Dare to do whatever God tells you to do and expect miracles to happen.

How busy are you?   Will you find room for God in your life?   Only if you want miracles to happen. Think, believe, dream, and dare... and you'll never be the same again.

15
Who Are You?

During Jesus' baptism by John the Baptist (Matthew 3:16), "Suddenly the sky opened and the spirit of God descended like a dove and hovered over him. A voice from the heavens said, 'This is my beloved son. My favor rests on him.' "

Think about this, Jesus had not yet begun his ministry. And God said, "You are my beloved. On you my favor rests." The word favor means to be pleasing to – "You are my beloved son in whom I am well pleased". We can stretch this a bit more as another word for pleased is delighted. "You are my beloved in you I am delighted".

God used baptism to cleanse Jesus' thoughts of who he was - he was not just a carpenter's son. God used the occasion to make it clear to Jesus and all those around that God was delighted in Jesus.

Let's be clear. This is before Jesus did one miracle, before he called the twelve, before he fasted for 40 days, before he thwarted the devil's temptations, before he started his ministry.

God found great delight - great joy in him. Clearly, Jesus did not earn God's favor - Jesus had it right from the beginning. The good news is so do we.

Consider – just consider – that each moment of your life God is saying to you "You are my beloved child - in you I am delighted". No matter what your past, no matter what your mistakes have been, no matter how many mistakes you make, no matter what addiction or dysfunction. God says to you, "You are my beloved child - in you I am delighted." Can you feel the difference? Can you feel the loneliness subsiding, the illness lessening, the love growing? Can you feel the joy rising in you just knowing that you delight God, today, right now, this moment.

When Jesus was baptized all the people standing around the lake probably said, "Who is this guy?". And God answered, "This is my child whom I dearly love and in whom I am delighted". He didn't say this is a carpenter, this is the savior of the world. He didn't say meet the great healer or here's the great teacher. He said, "This is my child whom I love and this child brings me great joy".

What if Jesus' baptism symbolizes a cleansing of consciousness? What if God cleansed the mind of Jesus from thoughts of lack and limitation and by doing so cleansed our minds as well. God made it quite clear. It was not what career Jesus choose that was important, what was important was who he was. He was a beloved child of God. What if you did not allow another moment to pass by thinking that your career defines you? If Jesus had done that, he would have died a carpenter. It is not what you <u>do</u> that is important. What is important is who you are. And you are a beloved child of God.

What if Jesus' baptism is a symbol of the type of cleansing required for your thoughts of lack (if only I weren't so busy, tired, fat, out of shape, sick); and for your thoughts of limitation (if only I had more money, a better boss)?

Allow each moment to be a baptism which cleanses your thoughts of lack and limitation and listen as God tells you who you are: "You are my beloved child on you my favor rests. I am delighted in you."

What if Jesus became the savior, teacher, healer not because he was destined to, but because he chose to. He chose to believe that he was God's son. He chose to believe he was loved without condition and he chose to believe he brought great joy to God. Because of these choices he had the courage to save us, the wisdom to teach us and power to heal us.

When asked, "Who are you?" - how do you respond? Often we reply, I work at company X. I am a Y. But our answers only describe what we do. In Jesus' baptism, God makes it clear; what we do is not who we are.

Who are you? Will you choose to believe that you are God's beloved child and that you bring him great joy? Will you choose to believe God is delighted in you? Once your thoughts of lack and limitation are cleansed, and you believe you are God's beloved child, you'll begin a journey of teaching, healing, and saving...and you'll never be the same again.

16
What Do You Want?

"Ask, and you will receive. Seek, and you will find. Knock, and it will be opened to you. For the one who asks, receives. The one who seeks, finds. The one who knocks, enters." (Matthew 7:7-8).

There are many ways to interpret these words of Jesus. You could think of them as a prescription for prayer. Consider – just consider – if this is our prescription for prayer - we could be in trouble. Especially if we do not know what to ask for, if we do not know where to look, and we don't know how to knock.

Asking implies you know what you want. How many do? You probably know what you don't want -- you don't want to be sick, or poor, or alone. But, what is the one thing that would make you truly happy? Do you know what to ask for?

Seeking implies you know where you are going. How many do? Do you have goals for each day, which would bring you closer to where you want to be? Where is it you want to go? Perhaps it is not a particular location, but a particular career path, or a particular relationship. What is it you want to achieve? Do you have a plan to get where you want to be? Do you even know where to seek it?

Knocking implies taking action. How many have the courage to act now? Now, not at some point in the future, not next year, not next month, not when the kids are grown, or when you retire. Now. Do you have enough courage to knock?

Jesus' words are a prescription for prayer. The prayer though, is not for ourselves but for another – possibly a total stranger. How does this work? If you want to receive, you must ask it for another. If you want to find, you must seek it for another. And if you want to enter, you must knock and open the door for another.

Begin today to follow this way, this truth, this life changing formula. Tap into the presence and power of God within you and decide what it is that will make you truly happy. Then give it to another. Develop a plan to find all you desire. Then share it with another. Take action. Then open the way for another.

When you connect to the power of God within, as Jesus did, miracles will happen. When Jesus cured the blind, he saw clearly. When he healed the sick, he was cured. When he fed the hungry, he was fulfilled. When he lifted up the dead, he rose again.

That old saying, what goes around comes around is amazingly true. It is not until we lift up others that we rise. It is not until we help another that we are helped. Blowing our own horn doesn't cut it. We will never be stronger making another look weak. We are all connected. We move as one body. When you give all good things to others, you draw all good things to yourself. When you show others the way, your path is suddenly made clear. When you open doors for others, doors are opened for you.

What do you want? Whatever it is. Ask it, seek it, knock on it for another and it will come pouring into your life...and you'll never be the same again.

17
What Are You Afraid Of?

Fear is defined by Webster as: "a feeling of anxiety and agitation, timidity, dread, terror, fright, apprehension, panic. In Luke's gospel, each time fear is mentioned - it is always a prelude to a powerful message from God. The messenger always had to address the fear, to make sure the fear was not a block, but a step toward powerful action.

When the angel appeared, Zechariah (Luke 1:13) was deeply disturbed and overcome with fear, and the angel said, "Do not be frightened, your prayer has been heard".

When the angel appeared to Mary (Luke 1:30), she was deeply troubled and the angel said "Do not be afraid, you have found favor with God."

When the shepherds (Luke 2:10) saw the angel they saw the glory of God and were very much afraid and the angel said, "You have nothing to fear I come to bring you good news".

When Jesus told Simon (Luke 5:10) where to cast his fishing net and upon doing so their nets were filled to the breaking point, Simon fell at the knees of Jesus and said "Leave me Lord, I am a sinful man". Jesus responded, "Do not be afraid - from now on you will be catching men".

When it was announced that Jairus' daughter was dead (Luke 12:7) and that there was no need to bother the teacher further; Jesus said, "Fear is useless, trust is what is needed", and her life was spared.

Jesus teaching the Twelve (Luke 12:32) said, "do not live in fear, little flock. It has pleased your Father to give you the Kingdom". These are powerful messages. Life-changing messages. The messages in Luke's gospel are the same ones we need to hear today:

∞ Do not be afraid- your prayer has been answered.

∞ Do not be afraid - you give God great pleasure.

∞ Do not be afraid - you will have great joy.

∞ Do not be afraid - when you put out your net, when you reach for your dreams, miracles will happen.

∞ Do not be afraid - you will be lifted up over every problem, every obstacle, even death.

∞ Do not be afraid - the kingdom of God is within you.

What are you afraid of? There are many events happening in our lives to make us tremble with fear. You only have to turn on the news or read the paper. But, it is not the things that happen around us that we should fear. We should fear what happens within us when we stay afraid.

In Luke's gospel (Luke 12:4) Jesus tells us what to fear. "I say to you my friends: Do not be afraid of those who kill the body and can do no more."

Consider – just consider – the "body" Jesus refers to is the message you were sent to bring to the world. You are here, in this time, in this family, in this place to deliver a message that only you can provide. God needs you to bring forth the message. And Jesus is saying there is no need to fear those who kill or stomp on your message, your dream, your goal, your plan. There is no need to fear those who say to you "I don't think you should do that", "You can't do that", "You won't make it", "That is not going to work". There is no need to fear those people who do not support your message. Your message, dream, goal will survive the blows because the power of God is within you.

Jesus added (Luke 12:5), "Fear him who has the power to cast into hell after he has killed. Yes. I tell you fear him." What if Jesus meant, you could be your own worst enemy? Whenever you allow someone to block the message, take away your dream, when you buy into their fears, and decide to give up on your dream -- you are in hell and you put yourself there.

So, to re-phrase Jesus' words, when someone tries to kill your dream, fear not. It won't work because you won't buy into the fears of another, you won't allow your message to be blocked, and you won't allow your message – dream, to die. However, when someone kills your dream by filling you with apprehension, terror, panic, anxiety, failure, and you buy in, you become afraid and stay afraid. You give up, forget the power and presence of God within you, and allow your dream to die. This you must fear. Yes. Fear this. Because this is hell.

Jesus said (Luke 9:62), "Whoever puts his hand to the plow but keeps looking back is unfit for the Kingdom of God". Once you move through your fear, hear the message God wants you to give to the world, act on the message, focus on the power of God within you, there is no going back...and you'll never be the same again.

18
What Do You Expect?

Jesus tells the story of a master going on a journey (Matthew 25:14-29):

"A man was going on a journey and he called in his servants and handed his funds over to them according to each man's abilities. To one he disbursed 5000 silver pieces, to a second 2000, and to a third 1000. Then he went away. Immediately the man who received the 5000 went to invest it and made another 5000. In the same way, the man who received the 2000 doubled his figure. The man who received the 1000 went off instead and dug a hole in the ground, where he buried his master's money. After a long absence, the master of those servants came home and settled accounts with them.

The one who had received the 5000 came forward bringing the additional 5000. The master said, 'Well done! You are an industrious and reliable servant. Since you were dependable in a small matter I will put you in charge of larger affairs. Come share your master's joy.'

The one who had received 2000 then stepped forward bringing an additional 2000. The master said, "Cleverly done! You too are an industrious and reliable servant. Since you were dependable in a small matter I will put you in charge of larger affairs. Come share your master's joy.'

Finally, the one who had received the 1000 stepped forward. He said, 'My Lord, I knew you were a hard man, so out of fear I went off and buried your 1000 silver pieces in the ground.' The master exclaimed, 'You worthless, lazy lout! You know I reap where I did not sow and gather where I did not scatter. All the more reason to deposit my money with the bankers, so that on my return I could have had it back with interest. Take the 1000 away from him and give it to the man with 10,000.'

Those who have will get more until they grow rich, while those who have not will lose the little they have."

Consider – just consider – this story is not about material gain based on what we are given to start with; it is a story of the power of expectations. This is a story of how confidence in our abilities, rooted in the high expectations of a master, builds dreams. This is a story of how little confidence in our abilities, plus low expectations of a master, buries our dreams.

You see, the servants knew the master had handed over his funds according to their abilities. The one who received 5000 silver pieces knew that master had high expectations of him and he rose to those expectations. However, the one who received 1000 silver pieces knew the master did not expect much from him. Likewise, he did not produce much. He bought into the low expectations of the master and in fear did not even take the money to the bank so it would at least get interest. He did not want to risk losing it, thus he did not want to take the action required to grow the silver pieces. He just dug a hole, and buried it.

What does the master expect of you? God has only the highest expectations for us. The Bible is filled with stories telling us how holy we are, how loved we are, how important we are. There are stories that tell us the great expectations God has for us, and they bolster confidence in who we are. Typically, however, we focus only on the negative. We study all the stories that talk about how low we are, how sinful. We think God has given us only 1000 silver pieces because he doesn't have high expectations of us. We dig a hole and spend our life stuck in it. But, when we think this way, we couldn't be farther from the truth.

Review a few of God's expectations for us:

∞ You are the light of the world.
∞ You are the salt of the earth.
∞ Blessed are you.
∞ I have called you my friends.
∞ Anything you ask in my name I will do.
∞ These things and far greater will you do.
∞ All things are possible.

If these few messages can tell us of the great expectations God has for us, does it make any sense for us to have low expectations? Does it make sense to allow others to influence the expectations we have for ourselves? How many times have you been afraid you'd lose everything you have by taking a chance, a risk. The servant who received the 1000 pieces of silver accepted the low expectation his master had of him, refused to take risks, and he failed.

Only those who expect much will grow rich. Be like the servant who received the 5000 silver pieces. The high expectations of the master filled him with confidence, he took action, he took risks and he became rich.

What do you expect? Expect God to have only high expectations of you. Expect to take action. Expect to take risks. Expect your dream to grow. Expect a miracle ...and you'll never be the same again.

19
What Do You Know?

"Sir, if you will do so, you can cure me" the leper said to Jesus (Matthew 8:2-3). Jesus responded "I do will it. Be cured".

"Sir, my serving boy is at home in bed paralyzed, suffering pain, cure him" said the centurion (Matthew 8:6-13). Jesus said, "Go home. It shall be done because you trusted".

"If I can only touch his cloak. I will get well" thought the women with a hemorrhage (Matthew 9:21-22). Jesus turned around and said, "Courageous, daughter! Your faith has restored you to health."

In each of these examples and in many others we find the formula for prayer. Prayer is not wishing and hoping things will change. Consider – just consider – prayer is knowing that change will happen. Prayer requires knowing. Prayer requires action.

Knowing is not simply wishing, hoping, begging. Knowing is more than trusting, more than believing. When Carl Jung was asked if he believed in God. He responded, "No. I know God exists."

Psalm 46:10 (New King James Version) states, "Be still. And know that I am God".

Simply believing allows room for doubt to sneak in. The leper, the centurion, and the woman all knew Jesus would respond. Each of them knew – they didn't just believe. Before they asked they knew Jesus would heal them. Their knowing led them to action. All three knew they had to get close enough to Jesus to make their request known. Both the leper and the centurion spoke to Jesus. They did not use a lot of words. The woman said no words at all, she thought them, and simply touched his cloak.

Jesus didn't need to be convinced of the value of their requests. He didn't require special words, or repetition, didn't judge the importance of the requests. All he needed was for the one who made the request to know their requests would be answered and take action.

Here is the formula for making a request as experienced by the leper, the centurion, the woman:

Take action -- get close to God connecting to the spirit within

Ask -- (aloud or silently) as though you've already received what it is you are asking for.

Know -- your prayer will be answered someway, somehow.

Some think prayers get God to change his mind. Perhaps he will give us what we want, just so we'll stop bugging him about it. Perhaps our persistence will wear him down and he'll give in. But, Jesus said, "Your father knows what you need before you ask him".

There is no need to try and change his mind, no need to convince him that we deserve something we don't yet have. There is no need for repetition. God knows what we need. He knows.

God responds when, by our thoughts, words, and actions we prove that we know he will. We prove it, by knowing our need is filled, even if we see no immediate evidence of it.

The leper, the centurion, the woman all knew if they could ask him, or if they could touch his cloak, Jesus would respond. And he did.

What do you know? You know your desires are only as far from you as your actions, words, and thoughts. You know God is waiting to respond. You know all you need to do is think, speak, and act as if you have already received your desire...and you'll never be the same again.

20
What Are You Clinging To?

Jesus' followers were devastated by his crucifixion. After the burial of Jesus, Mary Magdalene went to his tomb, found the stone had been moved away from the entrance, and she wept. She thought someone had removed Jesus' body from the tomb and did not know where they had taken him. But, the risen Jesus spoke to Mary Magdalene (John 20:17) and said, "Do not cling to me."

Webster defines the word "cling" as to hold fast, to entwine, to stick, to adhere, to be emotionally attached.

What if Jesus wanted Mary to understand the crucifixion was not the end of the story, though it was the end of his physical presence?

Consider – just consider – Jesus was giving Mary the secret to a successful life, and let's work through "Do not cling to me" word by word:

DO NOT CLING TO ME

∞ Don't be stuck on what you can see and feel.
∞ Don't be tied down by your fears.
∞ Nothing outside of you will make you happy -- not even me.
∞ Choose to find me now within you.
∞ Choose to be awake and aware of the great power within.
∞ Do not cling to my physical presence.

∞ Let my physical presence go so your spiritual life can grow.

We don't have the same problem the followers of Jesus had because we did not experience his physical presence. But we cling to things we know are not good for us. We cling to things we think we cannot live without. These are exactly the things we need to let go. They are tying us down, stifling our growth.

DO NOT CLING
∞ Do not cling to old ways of thinking.
∞ Do not cling to negative emotions.
∞ Do not cling to each other co-dependently.
∞ Do not cling to your habits.
∞ Do not cling to your limiting thoughts.

DO

∞ Let go of trying to control or manipulate others.
∞ Go beyond the physical into the spiritual realm.
∞ Stand on your own two feet.
∞ Be awake and aware of the power of God within you.
∞ Know that the universe contains the answers you need.
∞ Spread your wings.
∞ Rise above all obstacles.
∞ Rise to meet every challenge.
∞ When you DO ...you'll never be the same again.

21
What Do You Need to Walk Away From?

"At dawn, as Jesus was returning to the city, he felt hungry. Seeing a fig tree by the roadside he went over to it, but found nothing there except leaves. He said to it, 'Never again shall you produce fruit!' and it withered up instantly" (Matthew 21:18-19).

It is not often we read of Jesus' anger in the Gospels, but in this story Jesus curses a fig tree. Isn't it hard to imagine Jesus cursing? When we do, we try to discount it by saying "Well, he probably didn't really mean that" or "That's just another story misinterpreted by the gospel writers."

Consider – just consider – Jesus did mean it. This is not a misinterpreted event. It is a moment in Jesus life, like every other, that provides a lesson for us in our lives today.

How many times have you wanted something and didn't get it? How many times have you needed someone and they let you down? How many jobs have you interviewed for that went to someone else? How many times have you wanted to do something but found too many obstacles in the path? How many times have you gone to the tree of life, and found it without fruit?

This happens to us all the time. Everyday. We think if we only do X then Y will happen, and it doesn't. For whatever reason, it just doesn't happen. The lesson is simple. Walk away. Leave your frustration, disappointment, and heartache behind. Watch them wither. Take all your positive energy, your hope, faith, courage, talents and direct your energy to another path, another job, another plan. Something new.

When Jesus curses the fig tree he shows us that it is okay to walk away from something, someplace, or someone that is not providing what you need. It is ok to walk away from something, someplace, or someone that is dragging you down, preventing your growth, stopping you from being all that you can be. The story tells us it is okay to give up and walk away.

What is the fig tree in your life that you need to walk away from?   Perhaps it's a bad habit, a bad relationship, a job you hate. Whatever it is – walk away, leave all the hurt, pain, disappointment behind. Allow the negative energy to burn itself out – to wither, unattached to you. Start in a new direction, filled with hope.

Bernie Siegel said, "Nothing ever goes wrong. God is re-directing you"[11]. Learn from the experience and go forth in a new direction.

When Jesus cursed the fig tree, he provided us with a pressure relief valve. Why didn't he just instruct the fig tree to bear fruit? Because there are things in life you just cannot force to happen. The universe has other plans for you.

You cannot make someone love you.   You cannot force the boss to hire you. You cannot make a tree bear fruit out of season. You can, however, walk away. Walking away is the pressure relief valve of our lives. It is one of the best lessons Jesus taught us. You don't have to be miserable, uncomfortable, stuck.

Walk away and know nothing ever goes wrong, God is re-directing you...and you'll never be the same again.

22
Why Are You Stuck?

Jesus told a story about laborers in the vineyard (Matthew 20:1-16) "...the owner of an estate who went out at dawn to hire workmen for his vineyard. After reaching an agreement with them for the usual daily wage, he sent them out to his vineyard. At midmorning he saw other men, and said 'You too go along to my vineyard, and I will pay you whatever is fair'. He came out again around noon and mid-afternoon and did the same. Finally, going out late afternoon he found still others standing around. To these he said 'why have you been standing idle all day?' They responded because no one hired us. He said 'You go to the vineyard too.' "

Notice, only the first group he hired had an agreement about their pay. The agreement was that they would receive the usual days wage. The midmorning, noon, and mid-afternoon group were told they would be paid whatever was fair. The late-afternoon group was only asked a question, "Why have you been standing idle all day?" After they responded, the owner sent them to the vineyard with no mention of pay.

At the end of the day, "The owner, tells the foreman, to call the workmen and give them their pay but to begin with those hired in the late afternoon". Those hired earlier knew exactly what they were going to get; a usual daily wage; a pay that was fair. They worked hard in the scorching heat and were content with their pay until they found out that those who worked less also received the same pay. Once they learned this they demanded more.

The owner makes his position very clear. He placed no judgement on the number of hours worked or the pounds of grapes picked. He treated everyone the same. He said to those hired early in the morning, "My friend, I do you no injustice. You agreed on the usual pay did you not? Take your pay and go home. I intend to give those hired last the same pay as you".

The owner honored his agreement with those hired first. The owner did exactly what he told them he would do. The first hired needed an agreement, a contract to prove they would get paid. They needed to make sure all the i's are dotted, and the t's crossed. They needed established boundaries, limits on what they would and what they wouldn't do, what they would and what they wouldn't get.

To those who were stuck, who stood idle most of the day, the owner's message was - you worked for me though we had no agreement. There were no established boundaries or limits. So the owner could be as generous as he wanted to be. The last hired were willing to take a chance. The last hired were willing to do whatever they could to get un-stuck. They were willing to trust without an agreement, without a contract, or rules. They received more than they hoped for.

Consider – just consider – God is asking you the same question about your life, "Why have you been standing idle, why are you stuck?" Why haven't you achieved all you can be? Why do you focus on your limitations?

Our response, like those hired in the late afternoon, is because no one helped us. No one showed us the way. No one thought we were worthy. The owner, like God, responded not with punishment, judgment, nor condemnation, but with an invitation. "Go to the vineyard".

The workers went willingly without questioning the benefits. They were willing to make a change, and to work with no agreement on pay. It was their willingness to change, to take action without limits, or the need, of an agreement on pay, that the owner rewarded.

What if Jesus used this vineyard story to show that God does not want us to stand idle, to be stuck? To help us get un-stuck God wants to be very generous. The only limits to his generosity are the limits we choose to put into place. What if God says to us, "If you require a contract, I'll give you one, but I prefer not to have one with you. A contract requires me to limit my generosity and it sets boundaries on what you can do as well. I want to be generous and so I prefer freedom, yours and mine. All I ask is that you be willing to do what I need you to do without an agreed upon reward?"

Jesus closes the story with "The last shall be first and the first shall be last." Do you want to be "first" or "last"? It is your choice. One is not better than the other. Both are called. Both are rewarded the same. Both are loved. Neither is left out. God intends to be generous to both.

The choice is simple. Choose to be "last" with no need for agreements or contracts and you will be free to do the work you have been sent to do without boundaries, and God's abundance will pour forth. There will be no limit to what you can accomplish. Nor any limit to what you will receive.

Why are you stuck? Even if you are in the late afternoon of your life, it is not too late. Don't stand idle anymore. Don't be stuck. Let God be as generous as he wants to be. Go to the vineyard. Take a chance. Allow God to be generous. Be willing to do the work God needs you to do without a contract...and you'll never be the same again.

23
How Confident Are You?

On only two occasions, Jesus healed with no crowd watching. In Matthew (9:27-31), two blind men came after him crying out, "Son of David, have pity on us!" Jesus said to them, "Are you confident I can do this?" "Yes", they answered. At that he touched their eyes and said, "Because of your faith it shall be done to you", and they recovered their sight. Then Jesus warned them sternly, "See to it that no one knows of this".

In Mark (2:40-46), a leper asked, "If you will to do so, you can cure me." Moved with pity Jesus stretched out his hand, touched him, and said, "I do will it. Be cured." The leper was cured. Jesus gave him a stern warning, "Not a word to anyone, now" and sent him on his way.

Even though Jesus asked them not to, the blind men and the leper told everyone of their miraculous healing. Though they disobeyed a stern warning, their cure was not affected. They remained cured. How did Jesus expect them to explain their sudden sight, their sudden freedom from leprosy? Pretend that nothing happened. Hardly. How did Jesus expect them to hold back their excitement, their joy? Pretend that it didn't matter. No way.

Why then did he ask them not to tell anyone? He had already raised a child from the dead, and cured a woman of a hemorrhage. He had cured Peter's mother of a fever, and expelled a demon, prior to the two miracles mentioned above. The whole community knew about Jesus' healing power. There was no way they could not have heard about him. Why then did he ask the two blind men and the leper not to tell anyone?

Consider – just consider – he did not want them to tell because the healing would overshadow their courage, confidence, and faith. He didn't want them to tell because he did not want to take sole credit for the healing. Each time great faith preceded the miracle; the miracle of the courage, confidence, and faith of the blind men and the leper. The miracle is not what happens outside of us. The miracle is what happens within.

Miracles are a two-way street. You have to do something. What is it? You must be confident that it will be done. The blind men's confidence plus Jesus' healing power gave sight. The leper's confidence plus Jesus' healing power gave the cure. One without the other will have no effect. He wanted us to know that to change the outer imperfections we must change the inner. We begin by changing our minds, by filling our minds with courage, confidence, and faith.

How confident are you that a miracle is right around the corner? How willing are you to participate? To Jesus, our actions are more important than his because our inner transformation has to happen first, before he can begin to work on the outer.

How confident are you that your life can change? It is your courage, your confidence, and your faith that begins the transformation. When the inner transformation begins, and miracles happen, realize that it is your faith and confidence in God that made it so. Tell the whole story...and you'll never be the same again.

24
Do You Want to See Clearly?

Remember the saying - Two men looked up from prison bars, one saw mud, the other stars? Two people looking at exactly the same scene – see totally different things. One positive, one negative. One up, one down. One free, one stuck. One unlimited, one limited.

Sometimes when we look at our lives we see only the mud, the negative, the down, the stuck, the limitations. Sometimes when we look at others we see only their faults. Whenever we look at life or others in this way, we are like the prisoner who saw only the mud. Do you want to see clearly? There is a way to see the stars.

Jesus made it clear (Matthew 7:3-5), "Why look at the speck in your brother's eye when you miss the plank in your own?" A speck is a small bit, a plank is a long, thick board. A speck is insignificant – a plank is significant. He goes on, "How can you say to your brother, 'Let me take that speck out of your eye', while all the time the plank remains in your own? You hypocrite! Remove the plank from your own eye first, then you will see clearly to take the speck from your brother's eye."

No wonder we don't see clearly. We've been going at this backwards. We try first to fix someone else. Then if we have time we try to fix our own lives. After all, it is so easy to point out all the faults of another, tell them what they should do, solve their problems. It's easy to tell them how they should be raising their kids, cleaning house, handling the boss.

It's easy to tell them how they should be helping you or loving you. When you go about this backwards, you are a hypocrite. Webster defines a hypocrite as one who pretends to be better than he is without really being so.

We are pretending to be better than we are without really being so, when we point out the faults, try to solve the problems, fix the specks of others and ignore the planks within. Jesus told us everyone else's problems and everything they need to fix are the specks of life. These specks are insignificant. They are barely obvious.

If you want to see clearly, first you must look within. If you want to see clearly, focus not on the specks of another, but on the planks in your own life. The planks are the long, heavy barriers you painstakingly built into the prison of limitation, doubt, and fear.

When you see your own planks and tear them down, you will see clearly and reach for the stars. The planks are doubts which need to be erased, so you can trust the limitless power of God within you. The planks are fears that need to be overcome with love, so you can know the presence of God in every moment. Whatever the planks are in your life, chisel them down, be free of them, so you can clearly see all you are to be.

Without planks in your eyes you will be able to see and hear God in each moment. You'll come to know that there is a valid reason for everything that happens to you. You will be able to see the positive, the joy, the glory, the stars. You will be lifted up. Then perhaps you'll help another without pretense and the word hypocrite won't fit any more. You will clearly see you are not better than another – but you will be better than you were before.

Next time you look at someone else and are tempted to find fault (specks) remember, first your own planks and devote your energy within. Whittle your planks down until they become specks, so you can see clearly to reach for the stars...and you'll never be the same again.

25
What's So Funny?

Is there any place in the New Testament that says "And Jesus laughed", or "And Jesus had fun"? The reason Jesus came was "so that we might have joy and have it abundantly". To bring joy, you have to be joy. He must have had a blast. Having fun is a great gift of God.

So why isn't it mentioned in the New Testament? Perhaps our early church fathers thought life should be serious and edited out the laughter and the fun. Or, perhaps fun was such a part of the life of the apostles they didn't think to include it in their writings -- assuming readers would know Jesus had fun.

In Matthew (11:25), Jesus says, "Father, I offer you praise; for what you have hidden from the learned and the clever you have revealed to the merest children". Consider – just consider – what has been revealed to the merest children is how to have fun. What was hidden from the learned and the clever is childlike laughter and the pure joy of having fun. After all, kids know how to have a good time. They just know. They play for hours. But the learned and the clever, though they were kids once, now they are too smart, too busy, too whatever to have fun. The learned and the clever bury fun under the seriousness of life. The pains hide the joy, the sickness buries the fun, the anger hides the laughter.

Jesus came to take away the pain and sickness and anger. Jesus came to heal us. Jesus came to bring joy. Jesus came to have fun. And have fun he did. He walked on water, he cured the sick, he raised the dead. Do you think he did these things with a frown? No way. That must have been great fun. His face showed it. He smiled, laughed and had fun all the time. So should we.

Fr. John Powell tells the story of a grade school teacher who was tired of the kids – year after year she faced a new batch. One day she found a note on her desk, "If you feel ok could you inform your face?"[12]. How often do we smile? How often do we have fun? How many of us are waiting for "later" to have fun? "I'll have fun when I'm on vacation", or "I'll have fun as soon as I get out of work". What if "later" never comes? The time to have fun is now. Today. This minute. Every moment. Every moment of life should be sheer joy and fun.

Jesus goes on to say (Matthew 11:28-30), "Come to me all you who are weary and find life burdensome, and I will refresh you". In other words, come to me, all who have hidden their joy, buried the fun, and I will energize you. He goes on, "For I am gentle and humble of heart. Your souls will rest, for my yoke is easy and my burden light." In other words, keep your sense of humor, and I'll fill your days with fun.

What is so funny? Everything. Why aren't we smiling right now? Because we think we should be serious all the time. Because we've allowed the seriousness of life to bury our joy. Why aren't we enjoying every minute of our lives? Because we forget that Jesus came to show us how to have fun.

It is fun helping others grow; it is fun healing all that is not well; it is fun trusting when things look bleak; it is fun rising above every obstacle and challenge; it is fun loving each other.

Keep your sense of humor and find something fun in each situation you are in, regardless of how serious it is, have fun, every minute of every day...and you'll never be the same again.

26
Why Do You Fail?

Ann Linnea wrote, "There comes a time in our lives when we are called to believe the unbelievable. If we allow ourselves to believe, we open the door to the infinite possibility of who we might become."[13] Will you believe the unbelievable or not?

Immediately after 5000 people were miraculously fed, Jesus insisted the disciples get into the boat and precede him to the other shore (Matthew 14:22-33). "As they went to the boat, he went up to a mountain to pray. At about three in the morning, Jesus came toward their boat walking on the lake. When the disciples saw him walking on the water they were terrified and said, 'It is a ghost' and in fear they began to cry out. Jesus hastened to reassure them. 'Get hold of yourselves! It is I. Do not be afraid.' Pull yourself together. Peter spoke up and said – 'Lord, if it is really you, tell me to come to you across the water'. 'Come!' Jesus said. So Peter got out of the boat and began to walk on the water, moving toward Jesus. But when he perceived how strong the wind was, he become frightened and he began to sink and cried out 'Lord, save me!' Jesus at once stretched out his hand, caught him and said 'How little faith you have! Why did you falter?' "

It must have been difficult for Jesus to understand why in spite of many miracles the disciples just kept right on faltering. Webster defines faltering as to act hesitantly, to show uncertainty, to stumble. In other words, to fail. We often respond the same way the disciples did -- we falter when things go wrong. If you lose a job, keep a job you hate, your spouse leaves, or a relationship ends. You think "I failed".

Consider – just consider – faltering, failing, is not such a bad thing. Of course, there is no question that believing the unbelievable is a better way to live. After all, it allows you to walk on water, to see the infinite possibility of what we might become. But this story reassuringly shows that failing is ok.

First, Jesus insisted the disciples do something they did not want to do. Second, when they were frightened, he hastened to reassure them, "It is I". Third, Jesus said pull yourself together. Fourth, Jesus responded and gave Peter what he asked for, by saying "Come". Fifth, at once, he saved Peter from drowning.

Faith is a choice. You are free to decide how much faith you will live by. You are free to choose how much of the unbelievable you will believe. The beauty of it is that each time we falter, we experience God. Yes, in the midst of our stumbling, our uncertainty, our faltering, we will know the presence of God. If Peter hadn't sunk, he would never have felt the outstretched hand of Jesus who at once – that is without delay – saved him. If the disciples hadn't cried out "It is a ghost" they would not have known how Jesus hastens to reassure.

Why do we fail? Because we allow our fears to overpower our faith. We choose to believe only the believable. We choose to believe what is outside of us is more powerful than what is inside. The good news is that in our uncertainty, and in our faltering, we come to know the infinite possibilities of what we may become. Our faltering opens us to the presence of God within.

We come to know that sometimes God insists we do something we don't want to do. We come to know that he hastens to reassure and to restore our confidence. We come to know that he wants us to pull ourselves together. We come to know that when we ask, he responds. We come to know that when we start to sink, no matter what the reason, at once he reaches out with an outstretched hand to save us. We come to know the answers we are seeking are within. We come to believe the unbelievable.

When you fail, believe the unbelievable...and you'll never be the same again.

27
How Grateful Are You?

"Keeping their distance, 10 lepers raised their voices and said, 'Jesus, Master, have pity on us!' Jesus responded, 'Go and show yourselves to the priests'. On the way there they were cured. One of them, realizing it, came back praising God in a loud voice. He threw himself on his face at the feet of Jesus and spoke his praises. Jesus said, 'Were not all ten made whole? Where are the other nine? Was there no one to return and give thanks to God except this Samaritan?' He said to the man, 'Stand up and go your way; your faith has been your salvation.' " (Luke 17: 11-19).

When you look at it closely this story is amazing. First, the lepers really didn't ask to be cured. They said, "Have pity on us". Or, in other words, have compassion on us. Jesus said to them, "Go show yourselves to the priests." That's it.

Would the priests have allowed the lepers to get close to them? Lepers were outcasts, separated, even the priests didn't have much to do with them. Yet, Jesus said "Go". Can you imagine the conversation the lepers had on the way to the priests? Suddenly, along the way, they were healed. Made whole. No longer lepers. Now the priests would help them get clothing, food, perhaps work, and going to the priests made sense after all.

But one of the ten, didn't quite get to the priests. Realizing he is cured, he backtracks to find Jesus, and to give thanks. Jesus says, "Where are the other nine?" Well, of course, he knew where they were, they were on the way to the priests – doing what he told them to do.

And then, Jesus says, "Stand up and go your way, your faith has made you well." All ten were cured on the outside, only one was healed. The outer leprosy was gone and would stay gone. Nothing would change that, not even their lack of thankfulness. But to the one who was grateful, who backtracked along the journey, to tell Jesus face-to-face how grateful he was – Jesus healed his inner spirit, because that is where true healing is always needed.

Outer appearances, the experiences that happen to us, are only part of the picture. Though the outer is healed, the inner may be decaying and rotten with negative emotions, thoughts of lack and limitation. How do you get rid of these?

Do as the one leper did and have an attitude of gratitude. No matter what is happening to you, in the ordinary and extraordinary events of life, in the good or bad, give thanks. Everything happens for a valid reason, a sacred purpose. Will you be open to it? Will you seek out the lesson? Will you grow through it? Will you give thanks no matter what?

Sometimes we need to backtrack along our journey and look at things in a whole new way. We need to find something to be thankful for each moment. Miracles are happening to us all the time. If you haven't experienced a miracle today, you are not paying attention to the God within you. There are no accidents, no coincidences. We really aren't much different than the nine lepers. We look outside of ourselves for help, we are fearful, we are worried, we are anxious. Like the nine lepers, we follow the path of others to find our way. We go with the crowd.

Following the crowd, following something outside of you only leads to frustration and disappointment. Jesus told the grateful leper to "Go your own way" and true healing took place. Now the leper knows God is not outside of him, but inside, and he can go his own way without fear, anxiety, or worry. He is free of lack and limitation. He has been made whole.

When you have an attitude of gratitude, you'll know God is within you, you'll go your own way, knowing all will be well...and you'll never be the same again.

28
What Do You Want To Be When You Grow Up?

Each chapter in this book has revolved around a question of life. The final one asked is, if you could be anything you wanted to be, what would you choose to be? If today, you had a chance to start over – what would you be? If you knew all of your life so far, was just a beginning, and the greatest part of your life is before you – what would you expect? Bottom line, let's face it, our age may suggest we are grown up, but we are still just kids. The best of our life is yet to be.

The road of life we find ourselves on has many twists and turns. Sometimes we don't know whether to turn right or left. Sometimes we hit one dead-end after another. Sometimes we walk. Sometimes we run. Sometimes we go backwards.

Go out in the woods, and lay down next to the trunk of any tree. Look up. Follow the trunk, and go off into each branch. Note that each branch divides into more branches. Can you see how much your life is like a tree? First of all, there is the solid trunk, a foundation – your spirit, your inner teacher, your higher power. Notice how each branch is connected to the trunk, then it goes its own path, usually the opposite direction of the trunk. Can you begin to see how each of our experiences is like a branch? No experience is the ultimate. Each leads to another. "If only I get this job". "If only I find the right relationship". You march down the branch only to find yet another branch nearby. Each a decision to make. With so many twists and turns, so many leaves fallen to the ground, there are no guarantees in life, just more branches. But oh, how we try to hang on, to cling, thinking that this particular branch is the only one and totally, unaware that another branch awaits "...something better is trying to happen"[14]. There is no end to the branches – no end to the tree. It just keeps growing. Though all the leaves fall off in the Winter, each Spring it comes back bigger, and stronger. So it is with us.

The question is "What do you want to be when you grow up?" and consider – just consider – your answer is "A tree":

I want to be a tree.

Rooted in the earth.

With a solid foundation I call my soul, spirit, inner teacher, higher power, or God.

I know that I am enough just as I am today, but that throughout my entire life one thing will be constant and that is growth. I will always be more tomorrow than I am today.

I am moved by the wind, I thirst for the rain. I long for the warmth of the sun.

I am free of worry. I may lose a branch during a storm, or be uprooted during a tornado, but my seeds are always present, and at least one (maybe more) will find a new spot to begin to grow again.

I am a spirit. My outer condition may change, but my inner spirit will live on no matter what. I change. I will be transformed each winter and renewed each spring. I know that I can never be the same again.

I let go. My leaves (hopes and dreams) come and go. I don't try to cling to them. I trust the process.

I bloom where I am. Oh yes, it might be wonderful to be in California, or Florida, or Alaska. But I am where I am today, and I'll strive to be extra-ordinary.

I find the kingdom within me. All the answers I need are within me. I only have to be still and be open to them.

I own my shadow. It is not by light alone that I grow. I grow also through the darkness that sometimes overshadows who I really am. I embrace my shadow. I know when the light of my spirit meets the darkness of my shadow, I am transformed. I grow.

I am never alone. I may be the only tree in a field but I am not alone. As long as life courses through my branches, the source of that life is with me. God is my source. Wherever I am, God is.

I rise. I am focused on growth. I keep my eyes upward, focusing always on what is ahead. The past is meaningless, what I did yesterday or what was done to me, will not prevent me from growing today.

I risk. I take chances. I venture out of my comfort zone. I let my leaves drop because I know they will come back better than ever before.

When I grow up I want to be a tree, yet, there is more I need to be:

I take action. Wishing and hoping won't bring change into my life. I take charge of my life attuning myself to the spirit within. How many times must I try? One more time.

I make a difference. This world is a better place because I was on the planet. I will make my mark.

I am happy. Not because of my outer situation, or circumstances. Not because of my family, my job, my car, my health, my significant other, or my age. I am happy, because I choose to be.

I love. There are no pan-scales in my love. I give my love freely. Not 50% as in, you do this for me and I'll do this for you. I give my love, without condition, all the time, giving 100%.

I make time just to be. I don't have to be running from one place to another filling each moment with one activity or another. I have developed an "unshakable relationship"[15] with myself, so I can simply be.

I remember who I am.   I am a child of God.   I am loved.   I don't spend my life looking for someone who will love me.   It is not that others won't hurt me, they can't hurt me, as long as I remember who I am.   I am secure knowing everything I seek is within me.

I ask. I trust in the universe that all my desires are fulfilled.   I manifest my destiny, by putting my hopes and dreams out into the universe, giving gratitude, and knowing that either what I am asking for or something better will come to pass.

I move through fear. I take the energy of fear and transform it into action.

I expect miracles to happen. There are no limits to what I can be. When I face obstacles, I know that they are in my path to redirect my energies, and so I welcome them, learn from them, and move beyond them.

I know.   I don't just believe.   Beliefs can be shaken by the winds of life.   I know.   I know I am loved.   I know I am free.   I know I am healed.   I know all I ask for is possible.

I do not cling. Negative emotions block God's energy.   I let go of all resentment, bitterness, jealousy, all negative emotions. I do not cling to outcomes, possessions, or people.

I walk away.   When something doesn't work out the way I thought it would, or someplace or someone does not provide me with what I need, I walk away. I recognize the movement of the universe and I leave behind all my frustration, hurt, and disappointment. I redirect all my energy to a new path, a new branch for my life.

I am responsible for my life. I won't fall into the trap of blaming everyone and everything for my situation in life. I can change. I can start over.

I am confident. I expect miracles to happen all the time, and they will.

I look within. I try and find what is in me that makes me feel hurt or angry. It is only by looking within that I see clearly.

I laugh. I do not take life so seriously that I forget to laugh at myself, at others, and at God. In each situation, no matter how serious, there is something to chuckle about. I know my purpose here is to have fun. I enjoy each and every moment.

I am grateful. I am grateful before whatever I ask for comes to be. I give thanks for each and every moment, for every person, for each obstacle, for everything.

I'll never be the same again.

Sources and Resources

I have referred to God as a "he", however, do not be limited by my reference. Substitute whatever name you choose...Abba, Buddha, Krishna, Mother, Higher Self, Internal Teacher, Jesus, Spirit, Soul, Sacred Self, etc.

Lynch, Reverend Guy. Every lesson given at the Church of Today, 1995-1997.

Course in Miracles. Foundation for Inner Peace. 1992.

New American Bible, Thomas Nelson, Inc. c.1971, unless otherwise noted.

[1]Bolus, Michael. Life Science Academy. Grosse Pointe, Michigan. 1996.

[2]Walsch, Neale Donald. "Conversations with God, Book 1". 1995.

[3]Walsch, Neale Donald. Speaking at the Church of Today, Warren, Michigan Sept 21, 1997.

[4]Brown, Les. "Leap and the Net Will Appear". September 10, 1995. Speaking at the Church of Today, Warren, Michigan.

[5]Augsburger, David. "Caring Enough to Forgive and Caring Enough Not to Forgive". 1981.

[6]Powell, John. "A Christian Vision: The Truth That Sets Us Free." 1984

7Powell, John. "Unconditional Love". 1978

8Lynch, Reverend Guy. In conversation, October 17, 1997.

9Brown, Les. "Leap and the Net Will Appear". September 10, 1995. Speaking at the Church of Today, Warren, Michigan.

10Vance, Mike and Diane Deacon. "Think Out of the Box". 1995.

11Siegel, Bernie. Seminar – "The Psychology of Illness and the Art of Healing", June 22, 1996, Church of Today, Warren, Michigan

12Powell, John. Audiocassette Series – "The Growing Edge of Life". 1982

13Linnea, Ann. "Deep Water Passage: A Spiritual Journey at Midlife". 1993.

14Morrissey, Mary Manin. "Building Your Field of Dreams". 1996.

15Chopra, Deepak. "The Path To Love". 1997

Cassette Series by Rev. Guy Lynch

How Much Love Can You Stand?
The love you want is available. Discover how to find that love and share it in the context of a healthy, mutually-satisfying relationship.

Finding the Good Life
Your perfect life already exists. Everything you want to experience and achieve is simply waiting to happen. As you reach new levels of spiritual awareness and demonstrate this understanding, you will discover the key to Finding the Good Life.

Change Your Life
Learn to keep the good flowing into your life by taking an updated look at the Transforming System™. Guy presents a fresh perspective on the principles of Master Minding, Goal Setting, Image Book™, Affirmations and Personal Inventory.

Fear: Your Invisible Barrier
If fear is a barrier that is keeping you from experiencing the life you desire, this series can help you. Whether you are struggling with minor anxieties or full-blown agoraphobia, you can learn to transform your fear into positive energy to begin an adventurous new life.

Empowered Living
Within us is a spirituality that is as unique and diverse as the markings on our fingertips. It's up to us to empower ourselves by realizing our true, individual spirit. Experience the rewards of knowing YOU as Guy guides you through the process of self-discovery.

The Bible Was Made For You-Not You For the Bible
Everything you need to know to achieve success and happiness can be found in the Bible- if you understand it's hidden messages. Guy presents a unique interpretation of the scripture.

TO ORDER CONTACT:
UNITY CHAPEL OF LIGHT
503 NORTHWEST AVENUE
TALLMADGE, OH 44278 PHONE: (330)-928-2108

Becalm Publishing, Inc.
Order Form

☐ Check Enclosed
(payable to Becalm Publishing, Inc.)

☐ Charge my ☐ Visa ☐ Mastercard

Exp. Date Required

Mo.	Yr.

Order _____ copies of:
∞ Wake Up! Awaken the Spirit Within and You'll Never be the Same Again.
ISBN: 0-9662795-0-X

∞ $12.95 (U.S.) each copy.
∞ Michigan Residents add 6% (x.06) Sales Tax
∞ Shipping/Handling: $3.00 for first book, $1.00 for each additional book.
∞ Allow 2-4 weeks for delivery

Ship To Address:

Name: _____
Street: _____
City: _____
State:_____Zip Code: _____

Fax or Mail Order to: Becalm Publishing, Inc.
P.O. Box 725378
Berkley, MI 48072-5378
Fax: (248)-288-6105